More

SKILLS OF THE ASSASSIN

DELVING DEEPER INTO HUMAN DEPRAVITY

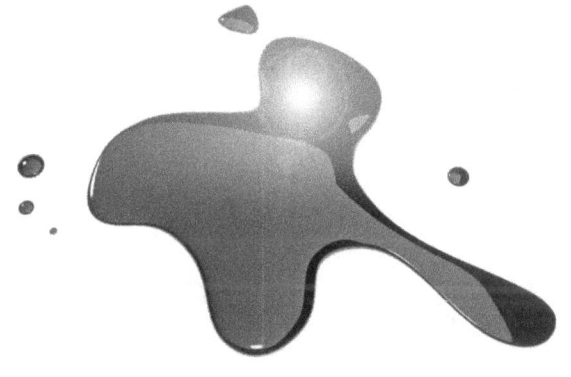

R.J. GODLEWSKI

More Skills of the Assassin: Delving Deeper into Human Depravity

Printed by CreateSpace Independent Publishing Platform
Charleston, SC.

Title page and chapter conclusion image: © deaff - Fotolia.com

ISBN: 1502421801
ISBN-13: 978-1502421807

TABLE OF CONTENTS

DEDICATION

To all who devote his or her life to defeating evil, wherever it may be found, and protecting innocent human lives wherever they may live.

ACKNOWLEDGEMENT

To God the Father, the Son, and the Holy Spirit – One God in Three Persons – without Whom I would find no talent, no opportunity, and no friends with which to affect either my trade or my interests.

Deo gratias.

ANOTHER BOOK ON ASSASSINS?

When *Skills of the Assassin: Understanding the Tactics of the Professional Killer* was released, there existed no comparable book on the market. There were, as it was previously pointed out, both books on *the* Assassins as well as individual killers, but none on the trade itself. Still, there were critics; individuals that for varying reasons decided to challenge the notion of a "book" on a secretive, sinister professional that rarely made the headlines. Others found inherent value in analyzing the trade as best as one could – even if it required tossing technical language in favor of a more colloquial approach towards communication.

Unlike, perhaps, the medical and legal professions, practitioners of security cannot isolate themselves into a clique of like-vocabularies in order to safeguard his or her career. National security represents too important a field to keep from the general population. After all, the horrific attacks perpetrated upon America during September 11, 2001 happened, in part, because differing government agencies failed to *communicate* segments of the treat to one another. Information *sharing* succumbed to information *hording* and the situation remains little better today. Arrogance represents the fundamental root of evil.

This book – as with the previous discussion on the skill set of professional assassins – is *not* written with such arrogance in mind. At least that is not the intention of the effort. On the contrary, people – *everyone* – bears a legitimate need to understand the variety of threats that may or may not confront his or her day. Naturally, assassins represent an extremely rare breed – even those under allegiance to drug trafficking and terrorist organizations – and therefore are unlikely to encounter your typical citizen. Nevertheless, the entire concept of *security* rests with leaving potentialities open. Very few, before 9/11, feared airliners crashing into crowded office buildings. Yet, if United Airlines Flight 93 was diverted because its brave passengers heard of what was happening, what *could* have happened to the other three aircraft if "someone" had read about terrorists using commercial airplanes as suicide bombs?

Skills of the Assassin was written for three primary reasons:

1. I wanted to write a book about a subject that no one had yet broached: individual, professional killers for hire;

2. I wanted to write a book that would stimulate discussion, even amongst critics, regarding a subject that most honest persons would consider simply too devious to talk about;

3. With the way that politicians are manhandling their constituencies today, it will not be long before books such as *Skills of the Assassin* are banned from publication.

And *how* did these objectives fare?

In the first objective, there are, today, no comparable

books written on the *skills* of individual and independent assassins. Every option consists of infamous assassinations, such as the John F. Kennedy killing, or narratives relating to how someone affectionately called *El dissector* found Jesus and is determined to set the record straight on his accomplishments. *Skills* was not intended to be an academic discussion of the motives, tactics, and case study repertoire of assassins. Rather, it was intended to place the context of the "assassin career" into the mind of virtually anyone who could read a book – for these are the people who cast votes, pay taxes, and, as in the case of the September 11, 2001 attacks, represent the "first observers" of society.

In regards to the second objective, *Skills* has fueled discussion and debate, especially since it has become recommended reading within several university courses within the United States and Europe. Some individuals like the book for what it is. Others absolutely hate it for what it was not supposed to be. Most, however, understood what they expected the book to represent and learned a thing or two about assassins that undoubtedly whets his or her appetite for learning more. And, under the premise of "what did you *expect?*", this book continues the discussion – for good or bad.

More Skills of the Assassin bears an appropriate subtitle: *Delving Deeper into Human Depravity*. This book moves (somewhat) away from the technological skills associated with individual assassins and discusses the mentality of the individual him or herself. Again, as with the original *Skills*, the subject matter "flourishes from chance meetings with some highly questionable characters and lifelong associations with the best that humanity has to offer. It rises from both formal academic study and informal personal inquisitiveness. And what you read [within the first book] remains a mere tip of nature's darkest iceberg." This new book digs far deeper into that peculiar chunk of ice.

Over the course of more than five decades, supported by an extraordinary – if somewhat independently minded – memory, the material within this book has arisen for whatever purpose you may envision. Some may find great value within its words. Others, perhaps, great evil. Still others may find the entire effort "childish" and unprofessional. Nevertheless, even the most elitist Special Forces operative can learn from, say, a housewife. At least that was the statement delivered to me from a former lead on a presidential security detail.

Nor am I claiming to represent anything "extraordinary" myself. Extraordinary individuals are those who give their lives to rescue innocent souls – even to love one's enemy" as it were. Seeing the world as it is today, I cannot imagine myself willingly dying so that others may destroy what God has given us. Perhaps, it is because of this that I have decided to write books on assassins and their trade. To keep the world aware of threats of all persuasions, especially those that remains so clandestine as to escape the attention of all but the most devoted moviegoers.

More Skills of the Assassin: Delving Deeper into Human Depravity is not a second edition of *Skills of the Assassin: Understanding the Tactics of the Professional Killer*. It represents its own book; a new volume, structured differently and possessing a novel perspective on the subject. It offers an individual narrative on how assassins may enter and actuate his or her trade. Only by understanding human *individuals* can we begin to understand their brutality, their resilience, and their seemingly indifference to killing...

R.J. Godlewski
Michigan
September 2014

CHAPTER ONE: *WHO* IS THE ASSASSIN?

Roberto always considered himself a normal American. By that, he meant, he was a decent Texan and never intended to harm anyone. Nevertheless, Roberto ultimately did not control his life – at least not its future. An average student with only one or two close friends, he joined the military and quickly became overwhelmed by the broader world that he was exposed to.

First, there was the shock of encountering new cultures and languages. Second, many of these new acquaintances held very little regard for the neophyte amongst their ranks. Finally, there were the brutal individuals that he met as he tried to escape from the first two confrontations. Instead of dealing with the indifference of his coworkers, Roberto sought new relationships that led to their abusing the green kid in ways often ignored by the general population. These transgressions forced the young man deeper into isolation and formulated a profound disregard for considering human individuals as anything more than mere occupants of the planet.

His inner aggression and subconscious desire

never to again permit another living soul to lay hands on him channeled him into maximizing his defense posture. That is, Roberto would strike first – before anyone could threaten his person or compromise his integrity. This desire to train and learn became an obsession. When killing – whatever one calls self-defense, the subject of taking human lives cannot escape attention – tugged at his sanity, he quickly changed his studies to include business, nature, and travel.

Because humans rarely ever forget things – permanently – Roberto's mind began to suggest that, perhaps, just perhaps, there was unity amongst these diverse subjects. One day, while lifting the weights that transformed him from a skinny Texas teenager into a well-contoured adult, it dawned upon him that there was money to be made in the business and marketing oneself as a weapon-for-hire. Roberto had thought long and hard about the consequences of this revelation, but the most intense thought that he had involved the apparent inconsequentiality of human life...

Science often engages within a feint, declaring that who becomes a criminal can be predicted with mathematical certainty. Yet, as soon as these social researchers reach his or her moment of clarity, an individual enters the criminal sector that literally shocks the academic and political communities. And, once again, the researchers return to their cubicles and laboratories to fathom some method of preventing criminality before it strikes close to heart.

Unfortunately, if sixty-five (65%) percent of the human population can inflict lethal force upon an innocent individual without more than severe orders from an authority figure in white lab coat and clipboard, those who engage within less destructive criminal enterprises must assuredly be greater than sixty-five percent.[1] For this reason alone, the individual *contract killer* remains, literally, indescribable. Nevertheless, most undoubtedly exhibit certain characteristics in common.

First amongst these attributes, as in the case of Roberto above, involve disconnect between the individual assassin and humanity at large. This does not mean that they hate society or cannot get along with other individuals. On the contrary, if one were to *hate*, then one concerns him or herself enough with the other individual to pay attention to their emotions, concerns, and personalities. Assassins do not observe human individuals surrounding them; they see only human *subjects* to be manipulated or studied. Manipulation serves to provide tools for the assassin's trade and study provides the killer with an opportunity to affect that trade. As often noted, *hate* simply represents another application of love (i.e., attention). Indifference, however, represents the true *evil* amongst society for indifference led to 1,500,000 Armenian Christians being killed by radical (former Ottoman) Islamists in 1915, 11,000,000 Jews and other "undesirables" killed during the 1940s by Nazi Germany, and 2,000,000 Africans decimated in Darfur during the present.[2] Hate may lead a disgruntled husband into beating his cheating wife to death, but indifference often leads to genocide.

Assassination, whether as an individual effort or committed on the premise of group dynamics, usually represents a case of indifference amongst the practitioner. Otherwise, the crime remains little more than "one off" murder, even if the individual represents a serial killer with

---

[1] Dave Grossman, *On Killing: The Psychological Cost of Learning to Kill in War and Society* (New York: Back Bay Books, 2009), 141.
[2] David Livingstone Smith, *The Most Dangerous Animal: Human Nature and the Origins of War* (New York: St. Martin's Griffin, 2007), 217-218.

several dozen victims under his belt. To kill for the sake of killing. To kill because of one's purest emotional or mental challenges. These are not the cold, calculated, and systematic killings of the individual assassin. Nor should assassins be considered as anything but the most conscientious of individuals – each within his or her own morbid way.

A comparison can very well be made with Islamic suicide bombers who often are considered by the uneducated as misfits and mentally challenged vagrants. On the contrary, suicide bombers are rarely insane individuals despite terrorism appearing to be an insane function.[3] In fact, at least one suicide bomber has represented a distinguished professional with a loving wife and small child.[4] Just because one individual may consider a thought or an action as "insane", does not mean that another *must be insane* to carry out that particular act. Otherwise, the world would quickly lock up most of the entrepreneurs inhabiting its surface.

In fact, it can be argued that most of human endeavors represent questionable risks undertaken by individuals. For this reason, many seemingly rational and stable individuals engage within dangerous sports to whet his or her appetite for experiencing danger.[5] Not everyone skydives, bungee jumps, or races automobiles for most would consider jumping out of a perfectly good airplane, trusting within an elastic rope as they leap off a towering bridge, or maneuvering through a traffic jam at 200 miles per hour as ridiculous.

Certain people simply function *better* within such

---

[3] Malcolm W. Nance, *Terrorist Recognition Handbook: A Practitioner's Manual for Predicting and Indentifying Terrorist Activities, Third Edition* (Boca Raton, FL: CRC Press, 2014), 12.
[4] Hala Jaber, *Hezbollah: Born With a Vengeance: Inside the World's Most Secretive and Deadly Organization* (New York: Columbia University Press, 1997), 1-6.
[5] David A. Grossman, "Defeating the Enemy's Will: The Psychological Foundations of Maneuver Warfare" in *Maneuver Warfare: An Anthology*, ed. Richard D. Hooker, Jr. (Novato, CA: Presidio Press, 1993), 151-153.

environments. Rather, they feel more comfortable, challenged, and, perhaps, *beneficial* within these dangerous pursuits. Our case study, Roberto, fused the premise of business and relative inconsequentiality of human life into a career path. His mind obviously considered the dangers and, possibly, the thrills of doing what no other rational human being would consider, but the ultimate consideration was largely one of utility: becoming an assassin represented the best way for him to pay the bills while expressing himself as a *person*.

On a recent television commercial for Tommie Copper®, a cowboy outlines the multitude of fractured bones and vertebrae that he often suffered during his bareback rodeo rides.[6] Nevertheless, this rodeo champion remains proud of his accomplishments and apparent fear of *losing* rather than dying. An irrational occupation? That remains a subjective analysis. Someone that would ride a 2,000 pound animal determined to destroy his or her body while they hope to survive for eight seconds may be just as "everyday" as another that spends a lifetime training for a "mere" eight-second taking of another individual's life.

Inasmuch as an Islamic suicide bomber believes that his or her murderous task actually serves a religious ideology, the individual contract killer believes that his or her function serves a practical side of human society. That is, they believe themselves to represent the ultimate precision-guided weapon destined to silence a troubling individual. Most, however, never bother to consider the definition of such troubles. Their trade largely represents an accounting one – the more individuals whose dossier is checked off, the more the assassin makes. Again, their business is baseline capitalism despite his or her particular niche representing a truly horrific one.

---

[6] See http://www.ispot.tv/ad/723w/tommie-copper-cowboy. Accessed September 2014.

From this, we can continue to isolate assassins from the general population:

- The assassin is a businessperson whose function remains to generate a profit from the provision of a particular service, almost exclusively on a no-cure/no-pay arrangement.[7]

- The assassin provides a lethal service, not merely a consultation or security arrangement. They are not "mercenaries" merely hailing to the highest bidder – but rationalizing and scrutinizing individuals who are not afraid to abandon contracts that prove too risky.

- The assassin remains a highly articulate and cultured individual – a "knowledge curator" – able to blend in with many different groups without raising suspicion.

- The assassin holds no special appreciation of the human species, but *does* devote a considerable amount of time studying human persons, particular his or her subject.

- The assassin lives within a highly controlled environment, whether partaking of his or her trade or hobby. *Everything* they do is meticulously planned and carried out – a byproduct of their trade.

- The assassin does not "stand out" either alone or in any group. Self-awareness permits camouflage within any environment or situation.

While not necessarily a revealing list, these attributes do suggest an individual that remains extremely rare within

---

[7] No cure/no pay arrangements – such as those used within the maritime salvage industry – dictate that no fees are paid until the successful completion of the service. In assassinations, this means *no money* until the deed is done.

society despite his or her chosen profession.

Roberto learned to distance himself from others, but his true revelation remained that he – and he alone – could combine his instincts, talents, and interests into *unity*. It did not matter that such unity involved appreciating his talents into systematic killing. Rather, his personal "essence" matured in a profession that few others accommodate. As the old saying goes, "there is always *someone* to fill a certain role, even as a proctologist."

With more than seven billion people on the planet, it remains inconceivable that no one will respond to a particular need or invent a new position. This alone guarantees the presence of assassins within the world. Nevertheless, we must delve deeper into the prospects of *emotionless* killers (Mafiosi and narcotics types are rarely "emotionless"). Even terrorists, such as infamous Weatherman operative Bill Ayers, feint growing out of their youthful "edge of certainty and arrogance."[8] Such statements suggest that the indiscriminate killing of innocent lives that defines terrorism remains a youthful indulgence.

The fact remains that several terrorist categories involve individuals as old as fifty to sixty-five years of age.[9] This dispels classifying martial individuals under any specific age bracket. Many terrorists – including some religiously motivated extremists – *might* be classified under the premise of narcissistic personalities: "people with a sense of entitlement, grandiosity, arrogance, a need for attention, and a lack of empathy or concern for others."[10] With the remote

---

[8] Quote cited in Ted G. Goertzel "Terrorist Beliefs and Terrorist Lives" in Charles E. Stout ed. *The Psychology of Terrorism: Volume I: A Public Understanding* (Westport, CT: Praeger Publishers, 2002), 110.
[9] Nance, *Terrorist*, 11-23.
[10] Michael J. McMains and Wayman C. Mullins, *Crisis Negotiations: Managing Critical Incidents and Hostage Situations in Law Enforcement and Corrections, Fourth Edition* (New Providence, NJ: Anderson Publishing, 2010), 313.

exception of the last item, it remains arguable on whether independent assassins bear any of these traits. The argument against compliance rests with the premise that narcissistic traits expose the individual bearing them and independent contract killers fail miserably if his or her identity emerges.

We will note that in Roberto's case, he channeled his arrogance and need for attention (as befitting many abused people) into what he conceived as an honorable pursuit, despite what the reader may visualize as either honorable or constructive occupation. This may simply represent a personalized approach to the "classical conditioning and social learning methodology" research the U.S. Navy conducted in the 1970s to aid military assassins in overcoming the natural reluctance to kill.[11]

Roberto's great revelation itself may represent little more than a human person's acquiescence to fate. That is, having had suffered terribly at the mercy of others, the assassin may subconsciously build a 'wall' around moral perception. As he succeeded in his chosen field, these revelations merely anchored his indifference to the task of killing other individuals. Independent assassins, by virtue of their trade, however, do not possess the luxury of *dehumanizing* their targets to empower hatred.[12]

Both Islamic terrorists and conventional armies, despite the breadth of their differences, can call upon primal brutality to defeat his or her adversary. Even in sports, such as ice hockey or football, we can see "classic rivalries" develop that permit teams to harp on their show boatmanship. Of course, such antics are largely a form of posturing – enlarging one's capabilities to terrify the opposing side.[13] Roberto would likely have lasted less than one day had he come back from an

---

[11] Grossman, *On Killing,*310.
[12] Ibid., 161.
[13] Ibid., 126.

assignment and bragged, "I just shot a banker today!"

Groups, such as the notoriously sadistic *Los Zetas* in Mexico bear the freedom to toss out the rules on ethical behavior due to their size, power, and relative lack of competition.[14] The same holds true for the Islamic State in Iraq and Syria (ISIS). The sheer terror imparted by either group remains shielded by their combined power to persuade. If, by contrast, Roberto operated as deviously, then his actions would draw the attention of prosecuting authorities. A beheaded business executive, for instance, would definitely draw the attention of the local media and – owing to the publicized exploits of both *Los Zetas* and ISIS – citizens alone would initiate charges of terror involvement.

In this regard, the independent contract killer remains the antithesis of terrorist groups: killing without raising either suspicion or terror. This further explains why Hollywood movies often grotesquely distort the actions of individual assassins – the need to captivate a viewing audience exceeds the desire to present a realistic depiction of the trade. Because independent contract killers, by definition, operate outside logistical and emotional support, they are bound to retain all information within the confines of his or her mind. This includes their presence.

In this age of iPhones®, miniature cameras, and instance access to YouTube® postings, it remains almost inconceivable that *anyone* would expect his or her life to remain relatively incognito. To do so requires extraordinary commitments to gauge one's interaction with society and expectations. Frankly, very few people in Westernized society are capable of doing so. This requires a conscious policy to avoid electronic communications, predictable habits, and

---

[14] George W. Grayson, *The Evolution of Los Zetas in Mexico and Central America: Sadism as an Instrument of Cartel Warfare* (Carlisle, PA: Strategic Studies Institute, April 2014). 26-27.

enforce culturally sensitive dress standards. Any contract killer – even one associated with a group – must be proficient in both camouflage and counterintelligence.

Like proverbial snowflakes, no two independent contract assassins are identical. That said, certain characteristics do present themselves as similar. While they may not lead investigators to *who* represents a hired killer, they can lead researchers to consider who may *not* be inclined to the field. Counted amongst other intelligence and evidence, deductive reasoning will begin to develop a sense of incredulity that, with inherent experience, single out prospects for further investigation.

These attributes are:

- *Desensitization towards killing.* Not to be confused with indiscriminate killing, contract professionals nevertheless represent individuals that kill systematically and routinely without it affecting his or her personality. Anyone can kill and many do so repeatedly. However, most of these "serial" killings expose emotional or psychological similarities that result in the killer ultimately being identified. Even exceptional examples such as the infamous Jack the Ripper involved a singular target: prostitutes. Assassins are not as exclusionary; his or her target represents more of a 'who' than a what. That is, they may target an individual from any group, any organization, any nationality, and any religion only to discover that his or her next target merely broadens their resume. To do this effectively requires an individual that *will not kill* unless they have accepted a detailed contract and then do so repeatedly and honestly.

- *Absolute discrimination in targeting.* Independent contract killers simply do not kill strangers. On the contrary, they may spend weeks and months gaining intimate details of that target's life, family, occupation, hobbies, health, and fears. They may come to know the individual better than that person's own wife, children, and even psychiatrist. While in fiction and theory an assassin may kill in order to survive, such is unlikely to be the case in reality. Part of this intimacy in understanding an individual's life rests with the need to commit the act without the killer ever becoming a suspect. Random killings – even those undertaken to survive another day – violate this condition. Indiscriminate murderers such as the Washington, D.C. snipers began their crime spree on the West Coast using methods dissimilar to their apex in the nation's capital.[15] Professionals understand that violating this rule by killing spontaneously can lead to capture through opportunistic prosecution. Years of meticulous planning can be decimated by *reaction* and, accordingly, any professional killer remains more likely to flee to survive.

- *A classifying personality.* Disorganized persons would *never* survive within the assassination business. The contract killer must keep an entire world of clients, targets, methods, cover identities, and business arrangements, amongst other personal information and responsibilities, within his or her mind for instant retrieval whenever required. This is not something easily affected by the casual citizen. Because of this, your independent assassin is likely an individual that can categorize many different subjects according to merit and priority as well as engages within various pastimes – such as music and collecting – that foster such capabilities. It is often featured that gang or group assassins engage within activities that leave paper trails (such as dossiers, communiqués, etc.) but this is not necessarily the case with the independent professional. Even amongst the arts, relatively few individuals can, for instance, catalog entire series of fiction stories for

---

[15] John West, *Fry the Brain: The Art of Urban Sniping and its Role in Modern Guerrilla Warfare* (Countryside, VA: SSI, 2008), 299.

future recovery. The professional assassin simply takes compartmentalization into an entirely new plateau.

- *Dissolution of modus operandi (MO).* Researchers have suggested that the frequency of variables regarding apprehension of criminals breaks down into knowledge obtained from detectives (79%), victims (48%), informants (23%), and the offender themselves (67%).[16] If we ignore the confusing ratios for a moment, we can determine the frequency of apprehension of "ordinary" criminals by his or her own actions that nearly match the supremacy of detective work. Part of these figures represents data collected from previous crimes or incarcerations. Unfortunately, assassins, particularly independent contractors, are not permitted *any* apprehensions lest they forfeit his or her identity (even apprehension on lesser charges runs the risk of exposing more about the assassin's trade). For this reason, especially, the professional contract killer represents an individual that simply does not fall into predictable patterns – a trait that likely excludes 99% of the human population.

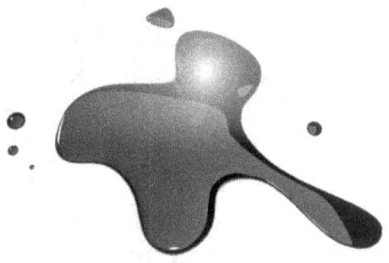

---

[16] Laurence Alison, "From trait-based profiling to psychological contributions to apprehension methods" in Laurence Alison ed. *The Forensic Psychologist's Casebook: Psychological Profiling and Criminal Investigation* (New York: Routledge, 2012), 14.

CHAPTER TWO: *WHY* ARE THERE ASSASSINS?

George emerged from a long line of Detroit gang members, his father and older brothers were members of the infamous Purple Gang and nearly every uncle served bootlegging liquor in one capacity or another. About the time that the notorious Purples – who served as the entire rhythm section in Elvis Presley's Jailhouse Rock – disappeared from the scene, the corruption and racketeering influence upon the young George had fully set its claws into the young Michigander. Crime, extortion, and, yes, even murder were not only common, but also expected.

Detroit had always been a particularly brutal city, more often than not ranking amongst America's top ranked murder capitals, and few others had witnessed federal paratroopers descend upon its ranks to squash urban unrest. It was in this capacity that George became a practitioner of the city's murder empire. At first, he became an enforcer of organized crime's infiltration of the state's many labor unions. When law enforcement and societal evolution took some of the bite away from organized labor, his bosses grew less enamored with his skills and by the time the 1980s rolled onto the scene, George the Enforcer became George the Entrepreneur, freelancing his trade amongst those illicit businesses that adopted their more reputable competitors' discovery of outsourcing staff.

With little need to protect turf, clients simply chose to reduce competition or informants. More than a few had wives' ex-husbands tinkering around too close to the backyard entrances. Having had grown up surrounded by institutionalized murder, George bore no qualms about continuing the trade on the side, even relishing the opportunity to formulate his own strategies and fees. After all, most of the people that others wanted dead were not the best elements of society. He was simply cleaning house a bit, removing trash inasmuch as the local garbage collectors of the Motor City. George had grown up surrounded by killing and why would he not capitalize on his "unique" talents and experience?

In the Biblical tale of Cain and Abel, Cain grew jealous of his brother's offering to God (Abel having received preferential treatment from the Lord) and tricked him out into the field where he then killed his kin.[17] It is always worth noting that this first recording of murder involved a religiously inspired crime, and one committed by a brother no less. However one categorizes the tale – historical fact or fiction – the parable remains true, for as long as there are at least *two* individuals around, murder can occur (suicide could still occur with less people).

This reality supports the much-discussed Dr. Stanley Milgram studies at Yale University during the 1960s; that 65% of the human population remain potential killers.[18] In George's case, the percentages were undoubtedly higher as they would be comparatively lower in, say, a convent or monastery. The reason that contract killings take place,

---

[17] Genesis 4:4-8 *New American Bible.*
[18] Grossman, *On Killing,* 141.

however, requires examination of the progression of society. At their fundamental core, individuals remain self-sufficient. It is only when they desire or require "more" are they forced to consider aid from outside parties. This, in effect, launches the concept of *trade*. For instance, a hunter may have spent his entire day tracking down the family's meal so he would not wish to waste precious time repairing or making his clothing. Therefore, he hired a tailor – perhaps bartering with meat – to provide the clothing that he needed to conduct the hunt.

Much of this trade developed when humans began to envision a sense of entitlement. Perhaps the hunter just did not *want* to do anything other than track game for a few hours each day. Maybe the tailor did not want to go through the gory details of slaughtering a deer, preferring to enjoy a nice venison stake without caring *how* it arrived onto his table. Here is where trade brings us the concept of murderer-for-hire. Let us presume that a prominent community figure, such as a banker or politician, wanted to benefit from the death of an individual but knew neither how to kill that individual nor how to do so without suffering the consequences of imprisonment.

To affect such a murder without care, all that the client would have to do would be to hire an individual that bore the experience of killing and the presence of mind to keep the client unconnected with the deed. For his or her role, the client simply had to envision a fee attractive enough for the assassin's time. In this regard, assassination becomes little different from bootlegging liquor during Prohibition – a product of supply and demand. Consider the parallel with casinos that have now proliferated throughout North America. Where once Atlantic City, New Jersey represented the only place on terra firma east of the Mississippi where individuals could legally gamble, now sit more than a few luxury casinos on bankruptcy row. The same could be said of divorces outside of Reno, Nevada.

　　While Abel's death in the Bible could be attributed to

Figure 1. Representative Examples of Popular Assassination

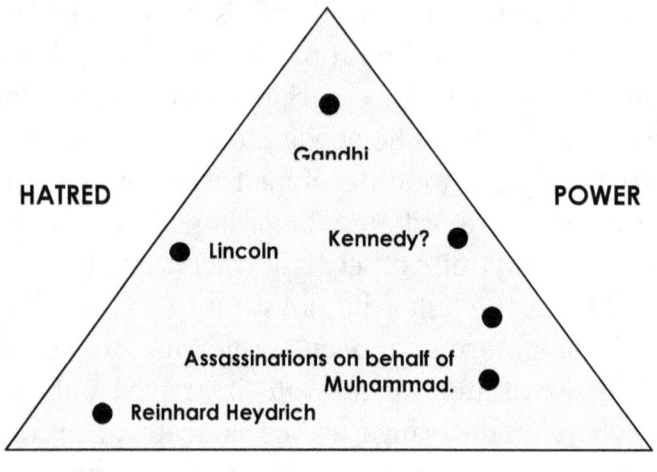

sheer jealousy, we can better explain it as hatred, which includes the sibling emotions of rage and resentment. Two other "excuses" flourish within assassination: revenge and power, perhaps the two most compelling reasons for an otherwise "respectable" person, such as a business executive or politician, to order the death of an adversary. Nearly every assassination on the planet can be positioned within the triangle of hatred, revenge, and power; some attributes more pronounced than others are. From here, we can begin to anticipate the *opportunity* present within such cases, whether the desired assassination arises from chance or even after a great many years of plotting.

　　We can further conclude that necessity remains a part of all contract assassinations, even if the client involved may bear a questionable need. If he or she is ordering an assassination, then *they* have perceived a need for the service. With these qualifiers in mind, we can apply the triangle of rationales to independent, contract assassinations, offering popularized historical case studies to outline the specific factors of private, for-hire killing.

The conquest of power – ultimately wrapped within the fabric of authority – represents the most valid argument for terminating an adversary. For the growing legions that believe that Pres. John F. Kennedy was killed as part of a broad conspiracy, there can be no rationale other than the expression of power by the conspirators.[19] The death of Mahatma Gandhi at the hands of Nathuram Godse certainly bore an equal measure of hatred. The Hindu fanatic desired no peace between his kind and Muslims and this suggests a sense of self-avowed power amongst Hindus vis a vis Muslims.[20] In the case of the Prophet Muhammad, his assassinations (committed either directly or on his behalf) drifted more towards revenge in his exercise of power.

In the context of raw power, Muhammad offered little tolerance for other beliefs. The assassination of ~120-year-old Abu' Afak and the poetess, Asma b. Marwan, who arose to herald his memory by composing "disrespectful" verses regarding the Prophet, attest to this.[21] The revenge aspect comes into play when Muhammad ordered the beheading of two prisoners as he "remembered their hostility and malice at Mecca."[22] It does not represent a significant leap of the imagination to view Muhammad's actions in context of the present era. Virtually any despotic ruler that cannot accept either tolerance or competition is likely to engage within

---

[19] West, *Fry the Brain*, 153-176.
[20] http://www.biography.com/#!/people/mahatma-gandhi-9305898#fight-for-indian-liberation. Accessed September 2014.
[21] F.R.C. Bagley, trans. *Twenty Three Years: A Study of the Prophetic Career of Mohammad by Ali Dashti*, 1985. 76-77.
[22] Ibid., 75.

martial justice.

On the opposite side of the triangle, we find simple hatred. Both Abraham Lincoln and Reinhard Heydrich – two diametrically opposed personalities by anyone's standards – were killed by persons who vehemently hated the leaders. John Wilkes Booth, the Confederate, thought that he could save his nation by killing Lincoln in a fit of anti-Unionist hatred. In Nazi-occupied Czechoslovakia, Allied-trained assassins relished an opportunity to kill the hated Gestapo henchman in order to save *their* nation even if both examples of assassins eventually paid the ultimate price for their efforts.

In the modern era, such hatred, revengefulness, and power seeking are not in short supply. Business leaders bloated with wealth, often seek to increase his or her authority by eliminating a competitor's key executive. Unethical politicians, hungry for further power amongst their constituents, may decide to eliminate a troubling journalist, investigator, or activist they perceive as standing in the way of their success. The possibilities are limited only by the sheer evil that encapsulates many lives.

Before one turns to assassination – usually – he or she must answer the following questions:

1. Will I escape connection with the murder, even after a great many years?

2. How trustworthy and experienced is the individual that I am hiring to kill my adversary?

3. Will the assassination actually *improve* my chances of affecting the desired outcome?

4. Will this deed place my own life (or that of my family) into jeopardy from revengeful persons?

5. Will I be able to live with myself after the deed is done?

It may not be surprising that procurers of assassination consider all but the final question.

When one broaches the subject of taking an innocent life (even if a very tainted one), they rarely give full thought to whether they could actually order the killing. Part of this, arguably, rests with the *emotional distance* between them and their target.[23] They do not *actually* commit the crime, therefore they may, on occasion, declare something to the effect of "Hey, the killer could have walked away. Therefore, *they* are the ones to blame..." A more powerful enabler rests with increasing the mechanical distance from the crime.[24] The assassin's client may never put much consciousness into the act until one day, a few weeks or months down the line, they pick up an evening newspaper to read about the "unfortunate accident" that befell a popular politician or business executive.

Even in today's prevalence of the Internet and high-speed communications, it remains unlikely that the procurer of assassination would bother to pay close attention to events. People are just naturally paranoid of exposure to crime and almost everyone erroneously concludes that law enforcement agencies always know what is happening or that crime scene investigation laboratories can solve the most dastardly crime within sixty minutes of prime time television. Nevertheless, the emotional and mechanical distances offered by employing contract killers remain sufficient for their presence to continue.

This permits the client of the assassin to release pent up hatred and revengefulness with the 'power' of escaping attention. When all works well, the professional killer becomes the ultimate guided missile with relatively little components to trace ownership and none of the intensity of, say, a suicide

---

[23] Grossman, *On Killing*, 156-170.
[24] Ibid., 169-170.

bombing. Regardless, the Achilles' heel of contracting for assassination remains the hatred-revenge legs of the triangle. Remember, Asma b. Marwan was assassinated on the orders of Muhammad because she resented the killing of an extremely elderly man, Abu' Afak. What we are discussing here is that one assassination doubled because *someone* learned of the first killing. And this does not rest solely with contract killers.

During the Plains Indian campaigns of the American West (1865 to 1879), both settlers and Native Americans engaged within one-upmanship regarding atrocities on a near-industrial scale.[25] Even uniformed soldiers were tortured in a way that would assuredly gain universal condemnation from today's United Nations (U.N.), including their having skin and digits sliced off.[26] These examples suggest the inherent hatred towards others within the human species, a need fully served by those who could care less about killing for profit.

Our case study, George, grew up within such a kill-or-be-killed environment and whether he was a Trooper George beheading an Apache or a Chief George ordering the tribal rape of a white captive and the murder of her infant son, the implications remain the same. [27] Killers exist because human beings *desire* killers. They may only quip, "Touch my daughter, son, and I will kill you!" without actually meaning it, but the underlying threat exists from periods such as the Plains Indian wars when tribes would often rape captured settlers five or six times merely on the way to fetch firewood.[28]

Empowering one's hatred and seeking revenge, assassins provide an opportunity for power, especially since the client may find the pleasure of being able to pick when and

---

[25] Thomas Goodrich, *Scalp Dance: Indian Warfare on the High Plains, 1865-1879* (Mechanicsburg, PA: Stackpole Books, 1997), 43-44.
[26] Ibid., 260.
[27] Ibid., 124.

if a selected individual dies. Compounding this remains the absolution that one experiences when committing murder as part of a group – even if that "group" consists merely of a client and the contracted killer.[29] Again, the client simply dismisses the action of murder as one of "*he* did the killing, not *me!*" in a vain attempt to avoid culpability. Much can be said of prostitution where many who procure the services of a sexual worker often deny the commission of a crime while simultaneously working to "rid the streets" of vice.

An assassin, in the eyes of his or her client, remains little more than a tool. Preferably one that no one sees or understands, but a tool nevertheless. Whereas George's former employers may have ordered dozens of killings, his own clients are unlikely to subscribe to the tactic any long-term value. After all, with each assassination the odds of becoming known increase with time. For this reason, too, assassins are less likely to accept assignments from repeat customers; it just compromises his or her security too deeply.

Privately sponsored killings are rarely more than "one-off" dealings. Those who desire such multiple murders are either psychopathic killers or under the tutelage of organized crime. Where independent contract killers circumvent this problem rests with the relative uniqueness of his or her occupation. Killing for revengeful businesspersons or on behalf of hate-filled and power hungry politicians requires an extremely prejudicial mind as each individual human possesses a completely different standard of enemies and adversaries.

The same assassin may orchestrate a murder in Bangkok for one particular client and then, a great many months later, facilitate another premature death in Doha for

---

[28] Ibid.
[29] Grossman, *On Killing*, 149-155.

an unfathomably different client, each bearing solely a personal reason for ordering the death of the opponent. Unless it bears some significance in planning, no respectable assassin questions "Why?" the hit is requested (though some assassins have his or her own manner in which to avoid those killings he or she may find "offensive" – inasmuch as contract killers can relate to *any* murder as offensive).

Perhaps assassins such as George never had a chance of avoiding their trade, but the real culprits lie with the money providers. Drug trafficking organizations (DTO) flowing across the southern border of the United States would not do so if it were not for hundreds of thousands of Americans freely paying for narcotics. Nor would politicians *anywhere* get away with siphoning funds away from constituencies if it were not for their padding the coffers of home districts at the expense of other communities. Assassins exist because killing represents a capital market run by entrepreneurs. Little more.

CHAPTER THREE: UNDERSTANDING THE ASSASSINATION *NETWORK*.

Bao-Jin was meticulous in her organizational skills, as was to be expected from her prior service in the People's Liberation Army Navy. Attention to detail in Red China often left less organized persons shepherded off to slave labor camps for the duration or otherwise "disappeared" into the mind-numbing bureaucracy of state apparatus. Nevertheless, Bao-Jin excelled in climbing the communist ladder – until she was assigned to managed Beijing's secret police activities in Panama where China had been accumulating maritime assets on a literal industrial scale.

Her overlords in Beijing were adamant about keeping their Latin American activities as clandestine as possible and Bao-Jin's role involved the liquidation of numerous obstacles to China's expansion. Maoist tendencies ran ripe throughout the region, providing the communist nation with eager pawns from Venezuela on through Guatemala. Bao-Jin's responsibilities largely concerned themselves with the Canal Zone on down into Colombia where exposure to various narcotics traffickers diluted her allegiance to communism a bit.

It was difficult to ignore the vast sums of money generated by illicit drugs and the lavish lifestyle of the traffickers, most of whom held little in common with the hardened communist bureaucrats she suffered underneath. After several years, the Chinese woman began to suspect that even her Beijing comrades were profiting from smuggling, a thought that tugged at her sensibilities regarding hypocrisies. It was when a Colombian smuggler made an off-hand remark about her own involvement in trafficking that began a long transformation of her life from communist loyalist to managing accounts of assassinations.

Like most entrepreneurs everywhere, Bao-Jin thought long and hard about her particular niche, having since decided to avoid narcotics trafficking itself as it would impose upon her bosses' profits and imply that Beijing did not take well to those who involved themselves in drug smuggling. No, she reasoned, she would need to find a niche less dangerous – meaning less noticeable – and yet as lucrative for a fledgling capitalist. After a few months of analyzing the situation, she began to detect an opportunity in killing-for-profit.

Bao-Jin could not help but notice the relative inefficiency of narco-assassins and realized that, although they bore the protection of such notorious groups such as FARC and Los Zetas, each individual's actions seemed to cry out "Catch me! I'm the killer!" to even the least enthusiastic police investigator. She realized that such actions bled the industry of otherwise capable "clean up men". With this knowledge in mind, Bao-Jin realized that she could aid her communist homeland by removing a few troublesome Westerners and build up some discreet wealth of her own.

Few can adequately understand what causes a person to involve him or herself into the business of killing for profit, but inasmuch as there are differences between personalities, there are different avenues to personal satisfaction. Regardless, whether one's chosen business represents, say, running a home improvement store or assassination-for-hire, *all* business enterprises involve certain functions that cannot escape categorization. Again, whether one prefers to transmit funds from a reputable bank in Zurich or through the personal intimacy of *Hawala*, each individual sets a standard of trust based upon that institution.

Despite the extremely covert nature of contract killing, both assassins and their suppliers, not to mention clients, remain connected through several nodes for which the astute investigator may uncovered with care. The modern criminal enterprise functions along both daisy chain and wheel networks.[30] These networks serve to facilitate and supply criminal enterprises, whether that involves narcotics trafficking or Islamic terrorism. Moreover, as with criminals in general, assassins benefit from *mētis* – the "broad range of practical skills that sailors, athletes, doctors, statesmen, and others use to respond to 'a constantly changing natural and human environment.'"[31]

Mētis provides the assassin with a sense of competitive adaptation that keeps him or her one-step ahead of law enforcement officials. Because contract killers represent a very literate group, their profession is not bound to approved doctrine. They may, for instance, employ "special operations" tactics when all suggests the need for amateurish flavor. Conversely, they may dupe police into suspecting a deranged killer when their specialization comes under scrutiny. They may read about a "one-in-a-million" accident and foresee it as a potential tactic. Routine may come into play when, for instance, staging auto accidents (assassins pay very close

---

[30] Michael Kenney, *From Pablo to Osama: Trafficking and Terrorist Networks, Government Bureaucracies, and Competitive Analysis* (University Park, PA: The Pennsylvania State University Press, 2007), 29-32.
[31] Ibid., 52.

attention to class action lawsuits).

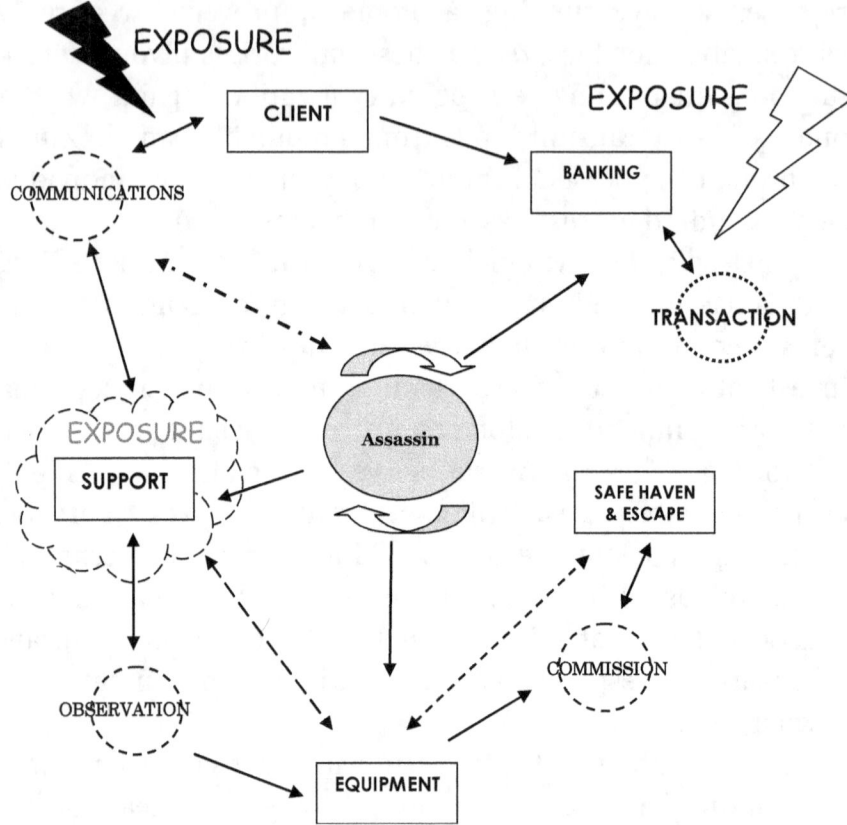

Figure 2. The wheel and daisy chain vulnerabilities of the assassin's network.

As briefly illustrated in the above diagram, the assassin's interconnection with society remains vague, but it exists nevertheless. Few if any individuals can move through the public without disrupting the flow of humanity. Most prominent of these disruptions include communications with clients, financial transactions involving commercial banks, and support from members of the broader population. All other nodes of the killer's network remain too apparitional to efficiently target (as with terrorism, contract killers bear the convenience of time whereas law enforcement agencies remain restricted due to budgets and employee shifts).

Bao-Jin's advantage came because of her presence within a state-centric bureaucracy that required documentation for every action. Sometimes, the best motivation for innovation involves intimacy with the "failed" perspective. That is, Bao-Jin likely realized that the Chinese approach did not provide value to independence – otherwise her superiors would not have been padding their wallets on the side. This does not require allegiance to capitalism, but it must address its appreciation.

In a similar manner, contract assassins may remain loyal to independence, but they must appreciate the presence of others who may or may not aid in their efforts. Mostly, if not exclusively, these public interactions are covert and none of the assassin's suppliers or benefactors understands his or her involvement. In fact, most individuals gladly contribute intelligence or other material support to virtually anyone who asks for it. Facebook® and YouTube® simply represent two such avenues where events, schedules, and videos are feely distributed.

After a few years' experience, the professional assassin can determine almost immediately which bars and nightclubs are likely to contain disgruntled employees, which thrift shops contain the right implements (all with compromising fingerprints), and which communities offer the best safe havens. Ex-workers, landlords, and even retailers all provide sources of information ripe for the picking by the astute killer well versed in the prospects of intelligence collection. And this intelligence fits immediately into his or her network for observation.

Only communications with the client and depositing of funds into a bank suggest concrete nodes vulnerable to attack. Every other activity undertaken by the assassin represents a nebulous maneuver difficult to intercept. Only banking represents the activity most likely to involve the assassin to some degree – at some point, the contract killer physically controls the transmission of funds whereas communications can *always* be undertaken through covert means. Here is where illicit networks expose their greatest vulnerability.

Because the contract assassin remains an *individual* profession, they do not benefit from layers of supporters, as would any other terrorist or transnational criminal group. Furthermore, there can be few "cut outs" to serve as a firewall between the killer and his or her supporters. This reality serves to isolate the assassin as well as increase the criticality of his or her exposure to apprehension. For example, when the Israeli government takes out an adversary, they generally have a group dedicated to cleaning the scene of an assassination. At a minimum, they bear a team that will ensure that the killers will make a clean getaway from the scene.

The individual assassin does not possess such a backup. This is why *their* actions are designed from the start to be as innocuous as possible. Their methods do not involve blowing up entire buildings or shooting up restaurants with submachine guns as would be the case with terrorists or governmental agencies. Often, they use the largely unobservant population as his or her firewall against detection. Furthermore, targets are either individuals that would not suspect attempts on their lives or people who expose themselves at predictable locations and times.

For this reason, the assassin's network may – repeat, *may* – utilize individuals that know they are working for someone of illicit character, but he or she will not know that their companion remains a professional assassin. Just *how* this remains accomplished is illustrated within the following scenario.

An assassin accepts an assignment to kill a local government regulator whose personal decisions caused a local corporation to lose millions through questionable environmental opinions. The company's president and prominent shareholder, unbeknownst to the board of directors and corporation officers, took the risky move under the premise that the municipal regulator's lieutenant offered a more attractive view of corporate growth. Furthermore, due to the lengthy time involved in locating a suitable contract killer – through rather nefarious means associated with foreign enterprises – voting the offending regulator out of office proved impractical. That the death of a government official, however seemingly "innocent", would cause everyone else to think about his or her role added to the decision.

The contracted killer, having analyzed the lifestyle of the official, determines that the individual's notoriety as a "pleasure drinker" remained sufficient to plan a killing utilizing the regulator's tendency to drink freely. This information was acquired by the assassin posing as a "former employee" of a previous business who wanted to dig up some dirt on the politician. The intelligence source simply believed that the "disgruntled" worker wanted to post derogatory information on a social media site.

Having had planned an unfortunate "incident" to befall the man, the assassin next turned to the local media under the cover of an "anonymous" associate of the local regulator and, having spent enough surveillance and intelligence gathering, presented just enough information to substantiate his story. This story, of course, presents the local regulator in a bad light. The reason for the anonymity, it is disclosed, is that the assassin himself partook in some of the illicit activities, but remains far too fearing for his 'family's safety' to go to law enforcement authorities at the present time.

It should be noted that the development of the newspaper story (more preferable than a television broadcast) placed suspicion upon the target. *Any* properly arranged death can be attributed to a myriad of causes, particularly suicides. In fact, the combination of a known drinker (who happens to possess a hostile character), allegations of impropriety (legitimate or otherwise), and an unexpected death do not ordinarily represent "assassination" in the minds of the average citizen, including government officials. In our example, the assassin merely has to orchestrate a murder that carries a "dual use" classification as potential suicide and overworked bureaucracies may not bear the time or resources to investigate another of the 6,000+ unsolved murders within the United States annually.

The above scenario, although exceptionally brief, is meant to illustrate the apparitional nature of the assassin's network. Each of the individuals identified within the example explored *knew* they were dabbling within illicit activity. The first individual aided an allegedly disgruntled employee, which *should* have raised concerns owing to the number of actual disgruntled workers that cause havoc. The second individual involved the press, which seeking a powerful story to print ignored the admission of criminal activity on the part of the assassin (as such happens all of the time for the media as any brief survey of Washington, D.C. reporting hints).

The third individual, not discussed but implied, represents the assassin's target himself. Each individual alive bears his or her own Achilles ' heel and the vast majority understand that he or she does *something* on the fringe of the law. The more powerful and public the figure – meaning, their ripeness for the clutches of an assassin – the more this paranoia focuses their behavior.

Bao-Jin undoubtedly worked this into her own intelligence network as her position within a communist bureaucracy allowed for her to understand which individuals were paranoid enough to prove useful. The hierarchy of capitalist-leaning communists is pregnant with individuals keeping tabs upon one another for covering his or her own backside. The nodes of clandestine, criminal networks (*all* criminal networks remain, technically, clandestine, but those involving higher-level crimes tend to be more so) do not possess definable edges. They represent storm clouds more than balloons.

With very little direct communication between the participants, the assassin's network remains more of an influential structure than even the daisy chain or wheel networks of transnational criminal organizations (TCO). In the TCO, you may have one or two lieutenants tasked with weapons and others overseeing intelligence. At some point in an operation, a "mule" is sent on an errand between the spies and the shooters. Often, communications are passive, but in the burgeoning world of advanced electronic intercepts, most organizations shift towards human couriers to affect their most clandestine roles. An example of this remains Syria's development of a North Korean-designed nuclear weapons facility. The site had escaped Israel's attention simply because the program employed hand-delivered communications exclusively.

The contract, *independent* assassin simply takes this a step further. He or she simply removes physical communiqués in exchange for carefully selected verbal commands that serve as a "cut out" should any particular party decide that there is, indeed, an assassination plot underway. For example, contrary to many Hollywood movies, there would be no "arms dealer" to provide the weapon of choice. The assassin does not need to orchestrate anything so elaborate to kill an individual. When firearms are employed, the considerations given trend towards non-discovery. For instance, sabot rounds in a rifle or a homemade firearm of one-off use. If the assassin possesses no mechanical ability – an assumed rarity by virtue of the profession – they simply do not employ 'weapons' requiring complex manufacturing processes. They do not fly to some overseas apartment building to meet with a black market arms dealer.

Assassination remains a business first. The bottom line is dictated by 1.) Profit, and 2.) Longevity. Only a fool conducts business exclusively free and idiots do not last long. This is why Bao-Jin's case warrants consideration. A stereotypical "middle manager" is not what the world expects of an assassin. Nevertheless, successful assassins are good at logistics and it does not present incredulity if many represent individuals such as Bao-Jin; people that can orchestrate a murder without, perhaps, *any* direct connection between the target and the assignment.

CHAPTER FOUR: SPECIAL OPERATIVE OR HUNTER-KILLER?

Ian spent his life in the wild. His earliest memories of childhood were of tracking animals across the veldt with his uncle and father. He knew, by heart, the tales of Hemmingway and the true life exploits of Jim Corbett and others that made hunting game the lifestyle for youngsters around the planet. Growing up within a world so large and unpopulated, the young Ian never spent much time worrying about the politics that grabbed the attention of the rest of the globe.

With few friends, and a continent as deadly from the wildlife as from the human population, Ian never learned to distinguish individuals as anything other than isolated members of society. True, there were blacks and whites, Dutch and British, soldiers and guerrillas, but hunting for food often made for strange bedfellows. Many of his guides were black and some of his clients were guerrillas that spent far too much time battling nations to worry about the trivial need of eating, so occasionally a lone paramilitary or small group would cough up enough money to pay for his excess meat.

As international politics began to solve most of the troubles from the previous centuries, Ian's original profession turned into stagnation as activists from all sectors began to interfere with his world and, before long, hunting animals became even less respectable than had hunting people. This irony did not escape his notice, for many of the individuals that infuriated the status quo came under the threat of those whose livelihoods they disrupted. These "paybacks" begin to interest the middle-aged hunter.

The ivory trade may have been since criminalized, but humans always found a way to legitimize – or, at a minimum, desensitize – murder. For Ian, it simply meant exchanging one career for another. After all, did not the world cull the herds or restrict migration of species after species for "the benefit of all"? With this at the forefront of his mind, Ian did not observe any distinction between good and evil, merely between useful and impractical.

Some confusion remains between the concept of "special operations" and an individual special operative, between the tools and tactics of the elite and the elite themselves. In *Skills of the Assassin: Understanding the Tactics of the Professional Killer*, it was argued "...people with the kind of military/federal training that *could* become assassins are observed with the greatest of care by domestic and international agencies."[32] This statement seemed to infuriate others who noticed references and images of "special ops" individuals adorning the book. Yet, the statement remains valid. People *known* to possess extraordinary capabilities are labeled as exceptional themselves and, therefore, remain expected to undertake outstanding service.

We witness a parallel within the security industry where a great many retired police officers and federal agents receive

---

[32] R.J. Godlewski, *Skills of the Assassin: Understanding the Tactics of the Professional Killer* (Charleston, SC: CreateSpace Independent Publishing Platform, 2012, 58.

employment or start companies of his or her own despite most professionals' recognition that private security and law enforcement remain diametrically opposed occupations. Nevertheless, most everyone – common citizen or experienced politician – naturally assumes that if they require security, then police and law enforcement personnel remain the best prospects to recruit.

Similarly, just because assassinations often require specialized techniques and training, does not automatically endorse recruitment from within the special operations community. Such prejudicial thinking illustrates why Army Special Forces, Navy SEALS, and U.S. Delta members are the *first people* scrutinized whenever something sinister occurs. Independent contract assassins *cannot* label him or herself as extraordinary. Again, the argument remains valid: such individuals remain scrutinized with the greatest of care.

Ian, to the contrary, possessed exceptional skills that today's younger special operations personnel would love to have. In fact, the realization of special operations as a panacea for global asymmetrical threats, the use of such special units has led to a crisis of manpower.[33] Recently, for instance, the U.S. Army paid $2,000 per day per soldier to train its infantry in the recognition and operation of Kalashnikov firearms. In the United States, virtually every firearms enthusiast understands the peculiarities of such rifles and the Kalashnikov collection within America is growing exponentially and training DVDs are available for one-tenth of what the U.S. charges taxpayers. Yet, not all of these gun enthusiasts can be considered "special operators" despite his or her superiority to soldiers in certain aspects.

What Ian offered his clients remains an intimate

---

[33] Sean D. Naylor, "The Spec Ops Stretch: Expansion plans leave many in Army Special Forces uneasy", *Armed Forces Journal* (November 2006), 30-35.

understanding of the natural world, something extremely valuable in the field of tracking human subjects. He possessed the patience, resiliency, and terrain appreciation that Western soldiers have lacked for over a century. It also remains a common misconception that an individual cannot track another as effectively within the city as within the wild, but this remains a fallacy. Sign located within an urban setting remains just as observable as evidence in the jungle. It merely takes a trained eye to detect.

Ian, as with all other experienced trackers, possessed the following skills.

- Patience and resilience;
- An acute and alert mind;
- Focused upon observation rather than seeing;
- An appreciation of terrain;
- An innovative and independent personality;
- A questioning character;
- A sharpened *set* of senses.

These attributes are required to wade through an environment no longer "natural" to the convenience-centric human being.

Experienced hunters also bear these qualities, though not as intensely studied as for the professional tracker. In the United States, hunting, as an art form, has become more of a seasonal subject rather than a generational one where, say, grandfathers and fathers pass on knowledge for younger generations to carry on. Tracking, because it remains a multifaceted skill – tracking lost children, fleeing terrorists, endangered species, etc. – requires a perennial commitment, advantageous for the contract assassin.

For their role, special operators, naturally, require their own special abilities. For analysis, we can consider the six mandatory principles of special operations missions:

1. Simplicity;
2. Security;
3. Repetition;
4. Surprise;
5. Speed;
6. Purpose.[34]

Two of these ideals are evident within *any* assassination plan and they are security and purpose. Of foremost concern to the contract killer, obviously, remains security. An ability to live yet again another day. Close behind has to represent the purpose of the contract for, again, "no cure, no pay" and such success requires the utmost in planning and purpose. No wasted thoughts or actions – *ever*.

Three others – simplicity, speed, and surprise – remain available on a case-by-case basis and the final principle, repetition, almost never comes into play for the simple reason that no two assassinations are identical and the assassin may not possess sufficient time to rehearse once an opportunity arises. Since assassination, on average, only considers one-third of the principles of special operations, contract killing *cannot* be considered as a special operation. Nor can the assassin be considered a special operative even if he or she may, periodically, take advantage of special operations techniques and technologies.

Based upon our considerations of hunting, tracking, and special operations, we can now conclude that independent contract assassins rest best be described as *hunter-killers* if we take care not to confuse either hunting as animal-centric or

---

[34] William H. McRaven, *SPEC OPS: Case Studies in Special Operations Warfare: Theory and Practice* (New York: Presidio Press/Ballantine Books, 1995), 8-23.

killing as a survival attribute. That is, the assassin *hunts* people and *kills* without psychological rationalization, effectively removing their association with militaries, criminals, or game.

Ian, in our example, simply applied his skills upon the plains into human enclaves because he never distinguished selected animals from targeted humans. In this regard, independent contract assassins *cannot* function in groups because, arguably, to form a complete break with humanity requires one to desensitize him or herself to mutual bonds, whether family, friends, or coworkers. This rests completely at odds with special operations units.

One of America's most notorious black units remains the Studies and Observation Group (SOG) of the Vietnam War. This operation heralded some of the most heroic actions undertaken by U.S. soldiers in American history. That said, the *bond* between soldiers within the units exceeded the expectations of the most honored fraternity. During moments of off-duty revelry, soldiers drank to excess, engaged within sexual promiscuity, and forced one another to tongue the ears of fellow soldiers.[35] At the extreme, a (future) Medal of Honor recipient willingly drank a mixture of ashes, human spit, nine alcoholic beverages, and stirred by a soldier's penis.[36]

Such behavior suggests that Western special operations warriors possess an "off switch" during which they can engage within behavior that would never be tolerated within society outside the war zone. Nevertheless, the contract assassin does *not* harbor these indiscretions nor are they privileged enough to have such 'free time' (as a sole provider, their security rests solely within him or herself and, therefore, cannot take time off). This further differentiates the independent assassin from

---

[35] John L. Plaster, *Secret Commandos: Behind Enemy Lines with the Elite Warriors of SOG* (New York: NAL Caliber, 2004), 34.
[36] Ibid., 74.

their special operations colleagues, as soldiers are only as good as his or her doctrine and command, which often shields or hides abhorrent behavior.

It took 30 years for the United States to honor the helicopter pilot that tried to stop the slaughter at My Lai during the Vietnam War.[37]   In the modern era, there are numerous soldiers, marines, and other special operators that have witnessed "immoral and unlawful conduct" but remain reluctant to talk about the travesties.[38] This during a period when militaries are forced to deal with "novel moral and political territory."[39] It may take 30 years, but *eventually* atrocities are ultimately discovered because, as in the case of My Lai, *people talk.*

Hunters, however, rarely commit atrocity beyond, perhaps, bragging about his or her exploits. Their lives remain too focused, too demanding to permit divergence, especially those tracking the most dangerous of game. Soldiers, for their role, often come into existence through the intensity of basic training and subsequent special operations schools. Hunters, to the contrary, absorb knowledge from both ancestral and maturational sources. These abilities come from *métis* – again, the "broad range of practical skills that sailors, athletes, doctors, statesmen, and others use to respond to 'a constantly changing natural and human environment.'"[40]

Young soldiers rarely learn from métis for only the most senior non-commissioned officers (NCO) spend enough time in the field to affect doctrine. Modern U.S. soldiers are simply

---

[37] Dick Couch, *A Tactical Ethic: Moral Conduct in the Insurgent Battlespace* (Annapolis, MD: Naval Institute Press, 2010), 29.
[38] Ibid., 3.
[39] Martin L. Cook, *The Moral Warrior: Ethics and Service in the U.S. Military* (Albany, NY: State University of New York Press, 2004), 79.
[40] Kenney, *Pablo to Osama*, 52.

not taught to function in tiny, self-contained groups.[41] The hunter, however, often has to function alone or, at best, in pairs to affect his or her trade. Even a common deer hunter may have to track a wounded animal for days in order to avoid sacrificing meat and effort. This diligence and "respect towards the animal" may be alien to many soldiers, even those of the special operations variety. As a tracker, the hunter is likely to have learned the skills from generations of ancestors before he or she is left to his or her own devices.

As an assassin, Ian certainly put his skills to work tracking human subjects. It provided him with an edge over competitors – such as they might have been – and made his scrutiny of unsuspecting targets all the more effective. Because they do live within a no-cure/no-pay world, assassins cannot retreat to base command, anticipate periods of liberty to endure penis-stirred alcoholic beverages, or retreat in disgrace as many non-Western armies do. They must "win" to survive – at least within his or her chosen profession. Defeated assassins either quit or end up dead or incarcerated.

Being a true Hunter-Killer implies a level of patience and resilience that few other humans can imagine. You are not simply planning a special *operation*, rather, you are engaging within a lifestyle mission where exceptionally rare targets remain scattered over several decades of "career" aspirations. Accordingly, the assassin *cannot* apply techniques exclusively but must rely upon tactics – an art and science dealing with the peculiarities of human maneuvers, both of the target and the assassin. This requires an inherent hunter mentality that, frankly, few military forces can muster. Even the best Special Forces soldier remains constricted by *time* – deployments, training cycles, enlistments, etc.

Consider, for instance, the targeting of a prominent

---

[41] H. John Poole, *The Tiger's Way: A U.S. Private's Best Chance for Survival*

terrorist leader by the forces of either the United States or Israel. Once a target emerges, the intelligence services of the nation may seek the whereabouts of the individual for years. When several likely locations are discovered, the military goes into pre-mission planning, selecting the personnel, training sites, likely methods of assault, etc. When both intelligence and military planning agree, the prospect for the assault is bounced back to the president or the prime minister for approval. At *any* stage between concept and execution, the entire mission may be terminated for a range of issues.

The independent assassin bears none of these layers and, therefore, functions as intelligence operative, tactical planner and political overseer homogenously. Furthermore, the contract assassin will likely have to analyze intelligence *and* tactics prior to accepting the contract. This remains one of the greatest fallacies of Hollywood, as no professional assassin would accept payment and/or responsibility for a killing that he or she did not work out effectively beforehand. It just would not make sense to place one's life (not to mention that of another's) in jeopardy without possessing a near-perfect chance of 1. Survival, 2. Success, and 3. Payment. Only fools rush in where professional assassins fear to tread.

Here, again, is where the qualities of a hunter bear merit. Successful hunters do not begin preparations on the morning of the hunt anymore than professional athletes begin training upon opening of preseason. To ensure a successful hunt, the individual spends weeks if not months calibrating his or her weapons, anticipating locations and, more often than not, 'feeding' the area to ensure that game remains likely to frequent the most advantageous location. In a similar manner, the contract assassin takes great pain to shift the probabilities of success into his or her favor. The selection of assassin tool –

(Emerald Isle, NC: Posterity Press, 2003), 3-18.

or, more correctly, technique – requires a great deal of consideration and planning to ensure that the assassination appears as anything but an orchestrated murder. The choice of location requires even greater attentiveness for to have an assassination appear "natural" requires a fundamental understanding of the target individual's lifestyle. This may require that the assassin lure the target into a particular location at a particular time by "feeding" the individual information or suggestions to make the killing more effective. None of these things is cursory.

In reality, the professional assassin may only possess three or four legitimate contracts within an entire career. This does not mean that the assassin's career represents a part-time occupation. On the contrary, the professional killer may spend several years seeking out the perfect contract (see next chapter) and then possibly another year to ascertain on whether that particular contract may be practical. The actual assassination itself may take most of a year to affect. With the potential period of any one assassination involving five years, the timeframe for four successful assassinations may take up two decades of a killer's life. Even for those assassinations that can be effected within twelve to eighteen months, they do not necessarily free up time for a subsequent list of targets.

The allure of hunting a target remains considerable for many contract killers. The process involves, insofar as possible, dehumanizing the individual through the process of simulating quarry.[42] The divergence rests with assassins coming to know every aspect of the target's life and, therefore, cannot escape the realization that they are killing a human *person* rather than an animal. Soldiers accomplish desensitization through a variety of methods, including referring to their actions as taking out, greasing, or mopping

---

[42] Grossman, *On Killing*, 254.

up the enemy.[43]

In taking down his or her targets, the contract assassin merely "closes accounts" as if an advertising executive merely capturing another fast food client. Whereas hunters proudly display trophies on den walls, assassins can only collect mental awards. It remains within the *tracking* of the target that the killer can shift his or her focus and thereby eliminate much of the "shock" associated with taking another human life.

Much as with their preference for disgusting beverages, many special operations soldiers (and normal grunts throughout the world) characterize their kills as "gooks", "Krauts", "Nips", or, today, "ragheads".[44] Assassins trend towards more corporate-like descriptors such as "targets" or "contracts" effectively legitimizing the assassin's business in his or her estimation. Hunting also implies a beneficial or survival necessity.

If only within his or her mind, the assassin remains simply a provider of solutions to nagging problems. A normal citizen would not – could not – spend 100-hour workweeks for months on end planning the demise of what was originally a complete stranger. In fact, most people do not know their best friend as well as an independent assassin eventually becomes acquainted with a target. Hence, the target morphs into *prey*.

Unlike military surveillance exercises, the assassin begins an intense scrutiny of the target's life and focuses exclusively upon that target, his interactions with the public, fears, hobbies, vacations, etc. This correlates with the image of the hunter-tracker stalking game across alien territory for that one opportunity to bag another trophy. In the case of the assassination, this "alien territory" may actually represent known urban settings, remote vacation lands, or aboard a

---

[43] Ibid., 91.
[44] Ibid., 161.

yacht in the middle of the ocean for that matter. Where, precisely, the target takes the assassin remains of little importance outside of determining the best location to kill the subject individual.

To affect his or her mission, the assassin must fully understand the psychology of the individual targeted, know intimately the environments likely to be transited by the victim, and possess a breadth of experience in how such persons could meet an accidental death. These characteristics parallel that of your typical hunter and the development of senses, intuition, and terrain appreciation are not learned from within books or taught within classrooms. In the case of Ian, his culture, heritage, and background provided a foundation few modern special operations soldiers bring into the military.

CHAPTER FIVE: *WHO TO KILL?*

Audun controlled a petroleum exploration and development firm in Norway, a company that had been associated with his family name for a great many years and, indeed, remained poised to develop into a significant supplier for the subsea market. Unfortunately, for the Norwegian and his company, a disgruntled executive sought to sell company secrets to a British firm and offered compromising marital information regarding Audun to blackmail him against going to the authorities. Desperate, fearing for his family's safety, and under tremendous stress to keep his company prosperous, Audun formulated a bold – and very much unethical – plan.

Knowing the offending executive's propensity for flagrant spending and suspicions of gambling debts with Russian organized crime, Audun decided to have the man killed by a professional killer, someone with a reputation for making "accidents" appear rather commonplace. Audun believed that the risks were extraordinary, but that given the circumstances, it was the only option to safeguard both his family and his company. That he would be ridding the world of a troublesome individual only eased the crisis swirling within his mind. Whatever ultimately happened to the Norwegian petroleum executive, the continuance of the company would benefit thousands of his fellow citizens and six children.

Given the nature of independent, contract assassinations, it remains extremely difficult to speculate on the recruiting process for the industry as a whole. Inasmuch as individual assassins bear his or her own reason for entering the illicit field, those who employ them bear equally diverse reasons for resorting to hired killers rather than employ more legitimate means to affect the grievances against his or her target. Conjecture is rarely beneficial, but before we even attempt to discuss how law enforcement and security personnel may be able to flush out assassins, we must envision the mindset of those that hire them.

Due to the extraordinary secrecy, planning, and money involved within private contract killings, we *can* rule out a great many deaths as victims of assassination. For example, a hostile housewife that works part-time in a grocery store remains unlikely to afford a reputable and skilled killer to eliminate her cheating biker husband. Similarly, a disgruntled client resenting a large bank merger is not the type to seek out a killer to dispatch the branch supervisor or even regional manager. These examples may very well represent people that truly desire death upon the offending individual, but their actions remain far too emotional for the cool, calculating, methods of the professional assassin.

So how, precisely, do clients recruit assassins? Frankly, in the vast majority of cases, it remains likely that the contract killer does the marketing. There rests no great deal of vision within this assessment, for *all* business people have to market their services and, well, the assassin represents a capitalist at heart. Furthermore, those in need of assassins remain unlikely to know of his or her presence and those who require such services more frequently (e.g., drug gangs, organized criminal syndicates, etc.) can be expected to bear their own internal unit for ridding themselves of unwanted personnel.

No, assassins do not advertise on television or through the Internet as if a modern day Paladin. However, those three or four lifetime contracts that we previously discussed allow – and require – for much time scrutinizing the opportunities that *may* appear from time to time. How, then, does the independent contract assassin market him or herself? For starters, they scout for pliable clients.

The assassin cannot rely upon either referrals or chance, so he or she makes a conscious effort to seek out the "right type" of person that could make use of his or her unique talents. Naturally, this does not mean handing out business cards or PowerPoint presentations. Yet, it does bear much in common with telemarketers that always seem to know *who* to call. Any marketing program – even a clandestine one – requires the researcher to focus upon specific models. We can ascertain an effective model for a professional, contract killer through presumption.

To begin our analysis, we can assume several key factors that *must* be on the mind of any contract killer:

✓ **The client must be able to afford the contract.** Contract assassinations are extremely expensive, which rules out virtually 99% of the global population. To achieve success within a one-off murder, an assassin must spend weeks if not months determining the life history of the target, the victim's inherent personality, and fashion a murder that bears a likelihood of escaping notice by some of the world's most advanced forensic laboratories. Arguably, this elevates the cost of any one assassination into the millions of dollars rather than "merely" a few hundred thousand;

- ✓ *The client must bear the ability for absolute secrecy*. Nobody gets away with *anything* if someone talks. If a client spends several million dollars to effect an assassination on an adversary, then it goes without saying that such an individual wants to "get away" with the crime or else he or she would gladly do the killing themselves. Furthermore, assuming that the client represents a business executive, politician, or other wealthy individual, then they likely have buried the payment for the assassination within a layer of licit obligations. Where the assassin bears a plan to escape culpability, the client unlikely has such measures in place other than extraordinary silence;

- ✓ *The assassination must affect an extraordinary outcome*. It remains hard to imagine a cold, calculating, systematic killer as a warm-blooded human person, but there is nothing to suggest that the contract killer of the sort representing the subject of this book does not bear scruples. After all, he or she is embarking upon an action that may ultimately comprise ~25% of their professional career. It is also entirely possible that "the future" effect of the assassination remains part of his or her justification. Killing a wayward husband may not be as rewarding as, perhaps, killing a despot. All people are vain to a degree and the assassin no less; he or she may enjoy sitting back in a comfortable retirement and reflecting upon how they affected the future of the world – even if only their little portion of it;

- ✓ *The assassination cannot target an omnipotent individual*. Contrary to Hollywood visionaries and conspiracy theorists, contract assassins shy away from targeting national politicians, prominent religious authorities, and civic leaders. Even a cursory examination of recent history proves that such murders remain in the public consciousness *long after the killing*. Professional assassins know that any targeting of, say, a national leader will trail him or her for the remainder of their lives. Therefore, he or she will remain targeting those individuals where the assumed lack of local law enforcement resources will benefit the assassin's escape. The death of a national figure, contrarily, will likely involve the investigative assets of the *nation*. An exception to this rule may be the murder of entertainers or athletes where "lifestyle" can absolve the assassin from more intense scrutiny.

With these basic considerations in mind, the assassin can scrutinize potential clients and broach the concept of murder through highly proprietary methods.

Each individual contract killer possesses his or her own methods for reaching out to clients, but they all factor in expenses incurred prior to the assassination, the relative importance of the target individual (and how much federal response will react to their killing), the likely benefit such an assassination will provide from the perspective of the client, and, of course, expected security measures throughout the course of the mission (See Figure 3).

Once these parameters are analyzed – though nothing is set in concrete at this early stage – the contract assassin can turn towards his or her preferred choice in isolating those potential clients that fall into *preferential* benefits from those that likely fall into *extraordinary* risks. All murders imply inherent risks, but the professional assassin does not represent a 'typical' criminal, as he or she has learned to temper violence in favor of a strict business arrangement. This fact simply magnifies their sinister profession.

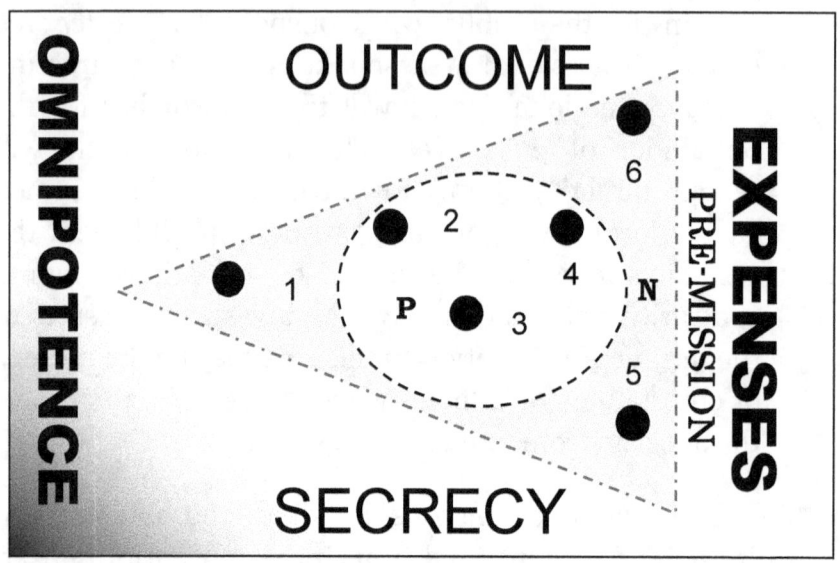

Figure 3. Representative clients. Key: **1.** National leader. **2.** Rogue scientist. **3.** Adversarial executive. **4.** Governmental regulator. **5.** Professional athlete. **6.** Entertainer. **P.** Preferential risks. **N.** Extraordinary risks.

In Figure 3, we can see a basic analysis of hypothetical targets. Towards the left side of the diagram, we can see individuals of exceptional importance such as national leaders. An assassination of such a client would remain extraordinarily expensive, hence the narrowing of opportunities. On the other hand, professional athletes and entertainers often lead lives that prove detrimental to his or her health. Thus, pre-mission expenses remain rather broad and recognized. However, there remains a broad divergence in mission secrecy and perceived outcomes. Rogue scientists, adversarial executives, and governmental regulators fall into preferential risks and costs. The regulator would diminish secrecy, while the rogue scientist would, by virtue of their infamy; require expenses that are more specific. Adversarial executives fall neatly into the middle of all considerations.

From this hypothetical analysis, we can see where the private assassin would benefit immeasurably from seeking out clients that wish to see certain executives disappear from the scene. In this regard, we bear not only a susceptible clientele, but also a rather large pool from which to peruse. How, then, does an assassin market to his or her client without drawing undue attention? First, we can legitimately assume that the assassin would remain detached from the subject.

If a businessperson wanted to develop marketing leads without discussing a newly developed product, that executive is likely to mingle amongst prospective buyers and *listen* to their concerns. He would be able to decipher which individuals are likely to purchase which products or services. Later, he could, possibly, analyze the group and see which people bore similar personalities or characteristics and then proceed into other similar patterned groups.

In Audun's case, it remains conceivable that the "ingredients" of his discontent were relatively known. Perhaps, he let his senior staff become aware of the rogue executive. These individuals may have spoken too freely during lunch or after work parties. Perhaps, the offending executive marketed his own "product" too freely, drawing the attention of bartenders, stewards, or lower level workers. With wind of a potential agitator, the contract killer could have begun to develop a mental dossier on the four requisites outlined above. Despite the seemingly 'million-to-one' chance of work being affected through this method, *time* is the one element that the assassin bears prior to accepting a contract.

He can afford to be discretionary with, perhaps, a $1 million contract to offset the million-to-one odds. Two key factors influence any potential client: survival of the entity or individual, and losses incurred due to the infraction. Many companies (e.g., in the telephone and beverage industries, consumer electronics, etc.) exist by virtue of a single product or service. This exacerbates the potential destruction offered by a disgruntled worker or renegade operative. All that the assassin had to do in the case of Audun was to float the idea that one human life was not particularly valuable in the context of a large company losing its cottage industry and several hundred people losing his and her job. All corporate executives remain bound to their shareholders even if the shareholder only represents the one executive.

With the seed planted, the assassin would have likely turned to magnifying the potential damage. Perhaps the assassin's first direct "contact" with the client materialized through the ruse of a journalist or agency regulator. This feint serves two purposes. First, it exposes the client to the reality that the crisis he or she is suffering through remains a legitimate problem, and not one solely within their mind. Second, it tips the paranoia scale in favor of suggestion. Audun soon began to realize that the problem was not going away and if he did not do "something", there would be hell to pay. All people, whether checkout lane clerk or chief executive, just want problems to "go away".

An assassin has now reduced the odds to, perhaps, one in several hundred thousand. He or she still has to work on the prodded client. The contractor, at this particular stage, could represent himself as a security consultant – one beyond the exposed crises of the company. He could offer his "team" to evaluate the situation and offer recommendations without the company's own staff becoming fully involved within the situation. This takes finesse, but assassination has never been for the weak hearted. Always, the client must appear to represent the one formulating options.

The client may not ever know that the person communicating with them represents the assassin that would ultimately take down their adversary. Several layers of deception are required but remain routine. Often, for example, a couple considering the purchase of a home may defer to a trusted advisor that may not truly exist. In this case, when a deal appears to sour, they can always suggest that their "advisor" did not approve of the transaction. Similarly, many women have feigned the existence of prior commitments to escape an unwanted date. The contract killer simply employs a similar ruse to escape direct one-on-one connection with the client's needs. This permits the assassin an opportunity to gauge potential clients without obligating or branding them with the task.

Again, the pre-mission orchestrations of the contract killer remain lengthy and full of trials and tribulations. He or she must find a secretive client with money and affect a murder that, in his or her mind, does not represent a waste. Those clients that openly seek to inflict harm are erratic at best and psychotic at worst. Furthermore, the assassin runs the risk of becoming a serial killer for these types of clients, where murder becomes not a force-multiplier, but a panacea for whatever ails the customer. This becomes deadly for all parties concerned.

The independent assassin offers a very brief association with any particular client: once the murder is affected, the client and the assassin part company *permanently*. Part of this rests with the singularity of the assassin's clients. That is, comparatively few business executives, for example, possess more than one adversary they are willing to have killed to avoid. Only organized criminal syndicates continually manufacture enemies. The rest of this short acquaintance remains fueled by the assassin's defense apparatus (see Chapter 6), that implies "death" if any client speaks to the authorities or becomes implicated in the death of his or her adversary.

This burdensome array of feints and dodges in relation

to recruiting a client and affecting an assassination simply represent a series of firewalls securing each move by the contract killer. These barriers – whether they represent the assassin posing as a journalist to inquire of trouble or as a security "professional" broaching the subject of proactive measures – remain little more than cut outs where the killer can walk away from the prospect without any illicit activity taking place or the client becoming fully aware of the who, what, why, and how of the proposed contract.

The further into the proposal client and contractor progress, the more nebulous the whole process becomes. In fact, the client may not *ever* realize that he or she is, in fact, funding an assassination. One could certainly envision a scenario where the "security consultant" promises an effective crisis management policy that inadvertently terminates due to an "unexpected accident" that prematurely took the life of the client's antagonist. A successful assassin will both kill without forensic discovery and enact a contract that pays a certain fee for *shortened* security contracts.

This serves two distinct benefits. First, it expands upon the prospective clientele of the assassin. Second, it eliminates the client from serving as a "witness" to criminal intent. Who would suspect a drunken executive falling off a horse and breaking his neck? Would not a suspicious client simply have the offender shot and killed rather than pay a million dollars for security only to have the problem solved by the agitator himself? Remember, professional independent assassins succeed because *nobody* can place a finger on their existence or methods.

This is why both *Los Zetas* and ISIS cannot deny their hand in assassination or the State of Israel escapes culpability whenever a building blows up holding a high-level Hamas or Hezbollah leader. Governments and terror groups are in the business of influence-through-violence and can withstand all but the most powerful public response. Contract assassins, however, cannot escape even the slightest notion of his or her occupation, which is why they conduct the utmost in planning and preparation. One mistake is literally fatal.

A client is hooked when he or she becomes "immune" to the assassin's choice of action, whether they understand that death of the opponent is certain or, perhaps, they remain naïve enough to fall for the "protective services" methods that opportunistically terminate rather early. The assassin's business does not flourish if they rely extensively upon the psychosis of prospective customers anymore than trial attorneys succeed if he or she waits for clients to discover the merits of lawsuits. Just that assassins, obviously, cannot advertise on television programs three times per hour nor do they engage within ambulance chasing.

Psychological profiling remains a taboo subject within the libertarian West, but contract killers remain expert in diagnosing an individual's mental state. They need to locate the right mix of instability caused by extreme stress and stability sufficient to remain silent over a potential crime throughout the remainder of his or her life. In this regard, most clients apparently fall within a specific age group: 55 to 65 years of age. We can only speculate on why this occurs – given no hard evidence or government figures to draw from – but it remains assumed that the correct mix of maturity, wealth, and power falls mostly into this age group.

Persons younger than 55 remain too social to keep secret and those older than 65 no longer control vast business empires or, perhaps, simply retreat into politics before retirement. Other age groups are too young to remain concerned about the success or failure of large organizations while persons much older than 65 have largely come to terms with life's adversaries. Exceptions always present themselves, but assassins remain mathematical creatures if only subconsciously. Contract killing remains risky enough without gross experimentation.

In summation, the professional and independent killer remains likely to decide *whom* to kill only after a complete and thorough understanding of who might want to eliminate another individual while maintaining previous ethical standards. This apparent irony remains valid as nearly everyone silently wishes death to befall another human being at least once within that particular individual's life.

Those who bear a lengthy list of unfortunate victims, again, generally carry out their own elimination requirements internally and do not possess a need for outside help. This singularity aids in the assassin trade as much as it does within that other infamous field of trial litigation. Very few people enjoy the prospects of going to court *until* he or she is swayed by a swift talking and seemingly rational "servant" of justice.

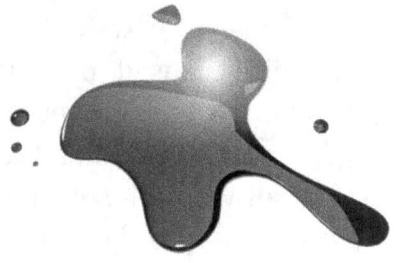

CHAPTER SIX: AN ASSASSIN'S DEFENSE APPARATUS

Kazimierz valued his retirement, coming after a great many years of political and social survival. The transplant to Detroit earned his "entitlement" the hard way – he spent most of nine decades battling those that wanted him incarcerated and those who wanted him dead. Mostly, they represented the same group. From his earliest memories as a child spy for the Purple Gang on through his many decades serving the auto unions, Kaz, as he was known to both family and friends, teetered on the precipice of calamity.

Despite the enormity of the alliances against him, Kaz knew that he had to have a personal security plan in place to keep the wolves at bay. This plan was simple and straightforward; whoever shall attack him would pay with incalculable costs. That is, Kaz learned very early that criminal adversaries remain too entrenched within their illicit lifestyle to fear danger. Furthermore, many of these villains protected their families with the best-armed personnel available.

Nevertheless, Kaz understood the fundamental weakness of security: the families of those protecting the Principal. High profile criminal and political leaders often bear the most experienced bodyguards and employ the latest available technologies, but these same executive protection personnel rarely could afford to protect his or her family as well as they did their client. Kaz simply leveraged his longevity with the knowledge that his adversaries could not expect that their protective services detail had not already been compromised, and this, in turn, forced the principals into spending far more time worrying about their continued survival from blackmailed protectors than worrying about this eager-to-retire-peacefully nonagenarian.

Kazimierz's security plan appears logical and many criminal elements have employed similar methods to escape incarceration or death. After all, what law enforcement or judicial representative would be willing to place his or her family on the line in order to go after a single villain? This represents little more than a theoretical application of Pablo Escobar's infamous *plata o plomo* – silver (bribes) or lead (bullets) – offering to officials in Colombia.[45] One can only imagine the security breaches implied by the numerous improprieties recently conducted by U.S. Secret Service personnel.

In practice, the policy remains highly effective: you do not target the 'boss', you target the loved ones of those protecting the boss. This rests with the guerrilla theory of attacking the least defended target and forms the foundation of asymmetrical warfare. As an assassin does not possess the infrastructure of other criminal groups, this may form the basis for his or her primary security perimeter: permit what public exposure you possess to ward off *any* thoughts of digging further. This, obviously, is not as simple as it sounds. For one thing, how does want spread 'terror' without arousing suspicion? For another, how does one protect him or herself from threats that, by nature of the business, are supposed to be apparitional to begin with? Finally, an assassin *never* works close to home and many – if not most – refuse to operate within his or her home country.

Much of this remains speculation, of course, but years of analysis and discussions (interviews never permitted) with some very unsavory individuals lead to the more noticeable. Since most contracts occur within foreign locales, the independent assassin cannot expect leniency if discovered. Even hardcore mercenaries *may* escape the death sentence, but only because they can hope to claim soldier's rights. Not the contract assassin; he or she is viewed as nature's most diabolical species and certainly would be made an example if discovered.

To safeguard against this prospect, the assassin works alone and survives alone. *Everything* he or she does remains controlled exclusively by them, even if some "luck" may enter the equation. Yet, by virtue of being a hired killer, some measure of notoriety aids in building this defensive plan required for survivability. Kazimierz endured the great difficulties associated with immigrating to the United States during the early industrial age and, like most Polish immigrants, his family had to land at Ellis Island as tough as nails. Add to this growing up within a criminal subculture that kept even Al Capone out of their territory and the new American could not have matured *without* a deep sense of "do unto others before they do unto you."

Kaz knew to keep looking over his shoulder all of his life. It became second nature to him as few things today come as naturally to his modern counterparts. Anyone that tried to

---

[45] Mark Bowden, *Killing Pablo: The Hunt for the World's Greatest Outlaw* (New York: Penguin Books, 2001), 24.

subvert or implicate him knew they were treading upon unsafe waters, for Kaz was known to possess some rather remarkable methods in dealing with traitors and the assassin must be just as ruthless in protecting his or her livelihood. In fact, this likely represents the *only* time when the independent assassin could benefit from attacking someone other than the target, the divergence from standard procedure representing a track to survive.

Before we discuss possible defensive plans to safeguard the assassin's career and identity, we must consider the key aspects of any such preparation:

- ◆ The plan must be communicated to all affiliated parties without directly implicating the assassin;

- ◆ The plan must be passive, implied more than stated;

- ◆ The plan must not lead to direct illicit activity or threat;

- ◆ The plan must be accepted as serious by the targeted individual;

- ◆ The plan must be eternal, without further input from the assassin.

These represent difficult, yet not insurmountable issues, and we only need to discuss briefly their presence. First, all parties involved must know the assassin's defensive plan. This includes those directly knowledgeable of the assassin's line of work (i.e., the client) and everyone remotely affiliated with his or her career.

Second, the defensive plan must be self-sustaining without undue activity by the assassin. That is, even when the assassin is sleeping or indisposed, the security measures must be effective. Third, the plan can "hint" at illegal activity, but it must *never* involve illicit harm. After all, the independent assassin has his or her hands full already shielding one of the most illicit activities on the planet. They do not possess time to add more to their plate. Fourth, the plan must *terrify* the targeted individuals into compliance. Nobody listens to those who they do not fear. Finally, the plan must be eternal, perhaps even surviving the assassin itself. Contract killers have been known to eventually quit or retire and even rear families.

With these thoughts in mind, we can begin to analyze a program that incorporates all these requirements. Several of these conditions rest with the inherent reputation accorded to a known assassin. Even if an individual does not understand that they are dealing with a killer, reputation rises exponentially with the suspicion of the subject individual. That is, a person may not know that the individual he or she is dealing with is an actual criminal, but the mere *thought* of illicit dealings remains enough to set their imagination on edge. The mere concept of authority – illicit or otherwise – remains enough to sway thought. Remember the 65% of the human race that can be induced into murder through a lab coat and clipboard.

The beauty of reputation is that persons not affiliated with the individual are not threatened by his or her capabilities. At least from *their* perspective, this accounts for every one of the conditions listed above. To foster this inherent reputation, the assassin merely needs to identify – without too many details – his or her experience. Again, the professional assassin is not seeking repeat business for to do so remains within the realm of *organized* crime. The independent contract killer rests best described as a *discretionary murderer* and their reputation rests upon discriminate objectives.

Today, during the 21st century, it remains difficult to

imagine *anyone* with the primal sincerity of the professional assassin. Even the term "professional" becomes overused and diluted. Both "professional" soldiers and athletes, as but two examples, fail on several counts of expertise. Often, the former is predicated upon technology and the latter, antics. With few extended campaigns to develop skills from – even the recent conflicts in Afghanistan and Iraq were considered "too long" to effectively combat, leading to ill-advised U.S. withdrawals – Western soldiers are forced to gain experience through 'ticket punching': diversity of experience, yet very little substance.

As for athletes, there are several prominent examples where the best teams of any sport – with allegedly the best talent and payrolls – remain defeated by upstart "Cinderella squads".[46] This argues that whether considering the U.S. military, the greatest military ever known to humankind, or professional sports, *reputation* often loses to lesser adversaries that bear not the reputation beforehand. Professional assassins, to the contrary, cannot sacrifice such reputation by privilege. He or she cannot allow Cinderella "teams" to compromise their security.

Kaz earned his particular retirement because those who knew him feared for the safety of their family should they ever desire to confront him. This "reputation" warrants considerable attention – especially within our politically correct-centric society of fearing to offend. This policy, itself, rests upon image rather substance. Consider, for instance, a press conference during a major crisis. Chances are, behind the podium stands a police chief or other high-ranking law

---

[46] For example, at the time of this writing, the 2014 Detroit Tigers baseball team with four consecutive division titles were swept in three games to the Baltimore Orioles who were in turn swept in the Pennant series 4-0 by the Kansas City Royals that finished second to the Tigers. Kansas City, prior to the series with Baltimore, swept the Los Angeles Angels, which had the best winning record in the American League. A low-salaried team that had not seen the playoffs since 1985 beat the two best teams in the league and passed their division champions.

enforcement official with a chest emblazoned with ribbons and medals. For what, precisely? Despite his or her devotion to protecting the population, are police officers comparable to a soldier throwing his body upon a live grenade? Do law enforcement personnel spend yearlong deployments in war zones? Not necessarily, but this suggests a public eager to see "authority" – remember the potential of 65% of your neighbors killing one another – in control of his or her life. Reputation is thus predicated upon *image* rather than action, much as how our most illustrious sports teams often fail under the spotlight.

Consider the following two individuals:

Table 1. Comparative Professional Personalities.

African Professional Hunter	American Police Officer
30 years experience leading safaris in Botswana and Zambia.	30 years experience serving the good citizens of New York City.
Reared on the veldts of Southern Africa.	Reared in Brooklyn.
Fluent in four languages.	Fluent in "street speak"
Hundreds of kills to his credit.	Never fired a shot in anger.
Able to spend weeks alone in the bush.	Leads a department of several junior officers.

Based upon the limited information provided above, *which* individual, in your estimation, warrants the greater reputation?

Much of this discussion depends upon the cultural expectations of the reader. That said, there remain vast differences between the two individuals described. The police officer, although obviously more publicly noted – and possibly decorated – has very little to authenticate his or her reputation. He or she lives within the same community they serve (despite differences in New York boroughs) and arguably rose through the ranks with relatively little 'danger' to disrupt his or her progress.

As for the African hunter, he may not have gained the public recognition of his American counterpart, but his experience covers a vastly larger territory and political system. His ability to communicate effectively also covers a larger cultural divide while he understands how to survive outside such communication. Most importantly, however, he *has* developed considerable experience in "life or death" decision making (see next chapter). At their most fundamental level, the police officer remains a servant whereas the hunter remains a killer.

In a western, urban environment, the police officer undoubtedly bears more respect and, possibly, admiration. Remove the uniform, however, and he or she disappears into oblivion in view of the uninitiated. His or her *reputation* depends upon those who know that their associate *is a police officer*. Outside of New York City, the police officer represents little more than a civilian with the "attitude" of a law enforcement official. That is, this particular individual bears all the training and experience of organized public service *without* the legal authority to carry on his or her function.

Although the great hunter of the Kalahari Basin cannot hunt Cape buffalo in, say, New York City, he is very much able to carry his personality forward in the city. He is undoubtedly familiar with survival outside modern conveniences and fluent in enough languages to survive within most urban centers he is likely to encounter. Where he excels over the police officer, frankly, rests with his *bearing* as a killer. Judge this statement by comparing photographs of a safari guide with a New York cop and you will notice the inherent differences immediately.

Dining, perhaps, at a local bar and the off-duty police officer will likely incur *some* respect, but the hunter will immediately attract a great deal of attention from those who, correctly or not, romanticize the profession. This *is* reputation and remains similar to what professional assassins likely receive from his or her clients. If there were some insane reason to do so, the professional assassin would gain more influence over a crowd if he or she shouted, "I kill people for a living!" than whether the police officer yelled, "I *can* arrest people in New York City if you break the law!"

This factors into the assassin's defense plan in two fundamental ways. First, the client is not likely to infuriate a person that he or she just hired to murder another individual with the capability of getting away with the crime. This would be akin to cheating a seasoned burglar of money. Only the fool would not fear retribution in kind. Secondly, *anyone* seeking to disrupt the assassin's career *has to consider* his or her own safety. Frankly, no politician or police officer is likely to tackle the killer without *significant* support – particularly if they know that the contract murderer can easily target *families*. And this brings us back, full cycle, to the original idea.

Politicians represent a different beast altogether for newspaper stories abound of disreputable examples sacrificing families for his or her career. Nevertheless, one can imagine the assassin possessing enough information – from his or her pre-mission intelligence operation – to offset any confrontation with "legitimate public authority". It does not take a leap of the imagination to envision Kaz saying, "Come after me and I will let the press know about the bribes that you have been taking" or, at a minimum, "*I* have been contributing to *your* election campaign, so do not even think about..." With minor alterations, such a policy would work in the assassin's favor.

For a professional, contract killer to function with any

longevity, he or she must ensure that they escape forensic investigation, which, despite the popularity of CSI-type television shows, does not require extraordinary measures. What the field does require, however, is common sense and exceptional planning. Law enforcement agencies remain cash-strapped and only the largest organizations possess any modern laboratory facilities. With minimal budgets and personnel, most police agencies tend to focus on the "obvious", or most public, crimes, which undoubtedly explain why there are approximately 6,000 unsolved murders within the United States during every year.[47]

The less obvious the crime – such as an elderly individual falling down the stairs or a known drunkard drowning in a swimming pool – the less likely law enforcement is going to divert substantial resources to the investigation. Suppose, for instance, an assassin were to conduct a rare killing using a firearm within a notorious area of Chicago's gang-infested neighborhoods on a Saturday night? Would the police even consider that, somehow, a professional killer orchestrated a murder after months of waiting for the target to transit the area at an appropriate time? Or would the murder be tossed onto the pile of drive-by shootings that have made the Windy City the murder capital of the country?

We can now begin to see how diligence works in with reputation to offer the killer a fair degree of protection from both those who *know* he or she remains a contract killer and those who merely *suspect* when enough information meets their desk. Add to this the well-known fact that the U.S. Federal Bureau of Investigation (FBI) only prosecutes when they have *a firm guarantee of conviction* and the reader can understand why they do not apprehend many professional

---

[47]   http://www.timesrecordnews.com/news/2010/may/24/unsolved-homicides/

killers. With no standard method, victims, locations, etc., it remains extremely hard to pinpoint any one individual as the killer of multiple victims. This leaves investigations to local law enforcement agencies whose experience and resources run the gamut from ridiculous to bureaucratic.

Much of this rests with the realizations that gone are the days when humanity viewed humans as anything but civil. Rarely, today, in the West, is there objective discussion regarding the brutality of the Plains Indians including their notorious scalp dances.[48] Nor of settlers who scalped Native Americans in turn.[49] Or of the often-too-many "pirates" that destroy the reputation of modern soldiery.[50] How this enters the discussion of professional assassins emerges within the context of there not being enough assassins in the world for anyone to write about them. Yet, just because some individuals remain unacquainted with the field does not preclude others from needing to learn about them.

In this regard, we can certainly make the case that *everyone* understands the concept of murder, for murder has been part of the fabric of humanity since the Biblical tale of Cain and Abel. If someone takes the pains to employ professional killers – whether organized or independent – then it cannot escape their attention that said professionals remain quite capable of killing *them* will little effort. After all, the subject remains, in the eyes of the public, a diabolical fiend with little remorse or restrictions.

When the assassin does emerge from the depths of secrecy to deal directly with other individuals (see Figure 2), he or she already bears a reputation of murdering at will – despite assassination representing a highly discriminatory

---

Accessed November 2012.
[48] Goodrich, *Scalp Dance*, 175-176.
[49] Ibid, 190.
[50] Couch, *Tactical Ethic*, 5-6.

profession. Nevertheless, we can ascertain what might constitute an effective 'defensive plan' founding upon the above. An assassin, building up his or her dossier on the target individual, includes a broad intelligence campaign regarding the client, his or her family, local support personnel, officials likely to affect the assassin's trade, suppliers, informants, and even media personnel. Anyone the assassin may come into contact with, used (even if the party does not understand they are being used), or come under threat of, becomes part of the general information gathering program.

Next, the assassin simply excludes the client from "how" the targeted individual will die or even "when". The client will know this information once the target enters the pages of the local obituary column. From this point onwards, the assassin simply states that *any* interference with the mission will result in severe reprisals (again not disclosed to the client). To safeguard this, the assassin may show photographs of the client's family to indicate sincerity (taken along with photographs of vulnerable law enforcement personnel).

If politicians are involved (or perceived as threats) a dossier on their family will be assembled for immediate disclosure should the assassin become targeted. Then, without fanfare, the assassin simply commits the crime and vacates the area. Simple? No, but you get the general idea. Assassins do not belong to a professional certification board. They exist for one reason only.

CHAPTER SEVEN: IT'S ALL ABOUT KILLING.

Roger resented being kicked out of the Army. He dreamed of being an Army Green Beret and spent his childhood pretending to serve in various locations around the world. When other kids were playing video games or talking with friends on Facebook, the young North Carolinian watched his dad's DVD of John Wayne in The Green Berets *several days per week, especially after his natural father passed away. His stepmother merely thought the young Roger's ambitions were simply part of the grieving process, but the U.S. Army learned otherwise.*

While not a terrible soldier by any stretch of the imagination, Roger's mental capacities were questioned almost immediately upon his enlistment. He bore trouble fitting in with his unit. Basic training nearly ruined his emotions and he required continual evaluation. Troubles rose and attitudes turned sour. Before his third year in the military, long after most of his compatriots believed that he would have been released for various mental impairments, Roger's mind finally let go and he attempted suicide when word arrived that his stepmother remarried and lost interest in communicating with the soldier.

With the fracturing of this latest straw, the Army

found no reason to continue his enlistment and he was released from his oath to serve the country he long since dreamed of defending. Or was it an oath of obligation?

Roger, upon his dismissal from the Army, an action that he viewed as dishonorable, sought to transform himself into an independent soldier. He would, he determined, develop into that most hideous of creatures – a soldier for hire without discrimination. No longer, would he serve simply for honor; Roger found a new niche that few other individuals possessed: an absolute indifference to human suffering or concern. Life, to the devastated ex-soldier, remained as inconsequential as religion to an avowed atheist. If humans could put down animals without much thought, he reasoned, why could he not put down humans too without much thought.

E ven the most decorated and experienced special operations soldier remains nothing more than a soldier bound to the laws and civilities of his native country. During the height of the Cold War, while U.S. soldiers were practicing with paper targets and straw-filled bayonet dummies, their Soviet adversaries were being trained to slit the throats of American airborne and Green Beret soldiers.[51] This remains representative of an American culture that views military training as "more of a policy statement than a source of warfighting procedure."[52] Such policy statements – of restricting warfare in some form or another – lead to troubles as in Vietnam where it took American infantry soldiers on the average of 50,000 rounds to inflict a single casualty.

It continues that Western-trained soldiers – and

---

[51] Paladin Press, *KGB Alpha Team Training Manual: How the Soviets Trained for Personal Combat, Assassination, and Subversion* (Boulder, CO: Paladin Press, 1993), 217.

primarily American ones – are not trained to kill as their more ancient brethren were. Clausewitz, who wrote, "war is such a dangerous business that the mistakes which come from kindness are the very worst", supports this statement.[53] Throughout this book, it remains posited that independent contract assassins, operating without any external support mechanism, *never* make mistakes from kindness. As we discussed within the previous chapter, they are not averse to targeting innocent families should their client – or the law – affect his or her primary business of killing.

From this brief understanding, we can conclude that such an assassin represents a calculated, emotionless killing machine that will not cease until either death or their decision to retire into the background. This presumption is based upon the conclusion that *anyone* experienced enough to kill – and kill repeatedly – without expectation of arrest would *not succumb to capture*. The reader should not expect any mercy from a government when apprehending what amounts to an industrial serial killer. Nor would the assassin.

Killing is definitely *not* a routine human action despite the prevalence of murder within human society. Some martial experts write that the slaughtering of animals may represent an efficient means of getting trained personnel accustomed to the taking of life.[54] This implies that even those individuals devoting his or her life to the pursuit of self-defense may find it unnervingly difficult to affect the killing of another human individual *without the external motivation previously discussed regarding the Dr. Stanley Milgram studies at Yale.*

---

[52] H. John Poole, *Tequila Junction: 4th-Generation Counterinsurgency* (Emerald Isle, NC: Posterity Press, 2008), 175.
[53] Carl von Clausewitz, *On War*. Edited and translated by Michael Howard and Peter Paret, (Princeton, NJ: Princeton University Press, 1976), 75.
[54] Rory Miller and Lawrence A. Kane, *Scaling Force: Dynamic Decision –Making Under Threat of Violence* (Wolfeboro, NH: YMAA Publication Center, Inc., 2012), 248-251.

In other words, the typical citizen, martial arts specialist, or professional soldier will likely not kill without the group absolution rules outlined by Lt. Col. Dave Grossman.[55] Most, if not all, Medal of Honor recipients, for instance, killed for the sake of saving *other lives.*

Even hardcore gang members and Mafiosi usually kill for the "family", whether through protection, revenge, or, perhaps, shock value. For their role and despite Hollywood popularity, elite military forces are not trained killers in the direct sense of the word. All branches of the U.S. military, as but one Western example, bear concepts of honor, integrity, commitment, or devotion within their statements of service core values.[56] If there remains *any* such statement for the professional assassin, it would have to include killing, secrecy, and survival exclusively for these represent the sole concerns of the individual contractor.

The smallest unit within elite forces possesses, to some degree, an "alpha male" that shepherds his team towards a "measure of individual honor and respect [which] extends collectively to fallen warriors."[57] This camaraderie and unit cohesion leads to such ridiculous escapades as the aforementioned instance of American soldiers drinking ash-contaminated beverages stirred with someone's penis.[58] Such actions, which would not be acceptable back in "civilized society", show the efforts that even elite soldiers must make to engage within killing on the battlefield. Undoubtedly, such antics involve a sense of posturing – "proving" that anyone brave enough to drink such concoctions are evidently brave enough to engage within combat.[59] This is simply magnified by group dynamics.

---

[55] Grossman, *On Killing*, 149-155.
[56] Couch, *Tactical Ethic*, 116.
[57] Ibid., 28.
[58] Plaster, *Secret Commandos*, 74.

In contrast, the contract assassin has to exhibit something best compared with the Japanese concept of *shibumi* – an austere perfection that keeps the "warrior" grounded into those simplistic qualities that pare away everything within an individual's techniques or actions that remains imperfect and superfluous.[60] The independent contract killer has to "fool everyone...all of the time" in order to survive within the world. This necessitates *eliminating everything that may appear suspicious or extraordinary for an individual to do.*

There can be no theatrics in killing for hire. No terrorism or fantasy in any contract. The assassin is simply a contract *killer* that does not need to gain the support of a squad, company, or terrorist cell. Beyond all else, this suggests apathy on an astronomical scale, for even religiously motivated jihadists often shout some Islamic phrase just before they blow themselves up or begin shooting at individuals. It remains arguable whether assassins even bear a hesitant thought before he or she orchestrates the death of another individual, for to do so suggests an evolving sense of remorse, something that is likely to terminate a career early.

For assassins – of the independent, professional variety – to exist, *something* has to influence the way that particular individual develops. That is, somewhere along the development of the human mind from basic survival to the complacency of entitlement, the natural progression evolved over eons must have ceased. Here is where an individual no longer cares about society building or cooperation. He or she simply rests within that brief pause between competitive/aggressive behavior and the alliance building, cooperative phase that exists just before society building can

---

[59] Grossman, *On Killing*, 5-9.
[60] Forrest E. Morgan, *Living the Martial Way: A Manual for the Way a Modern Warrior Should Think* (Fort Lee, NJ: Barricade Books, 1992), 270-274.

take hold.

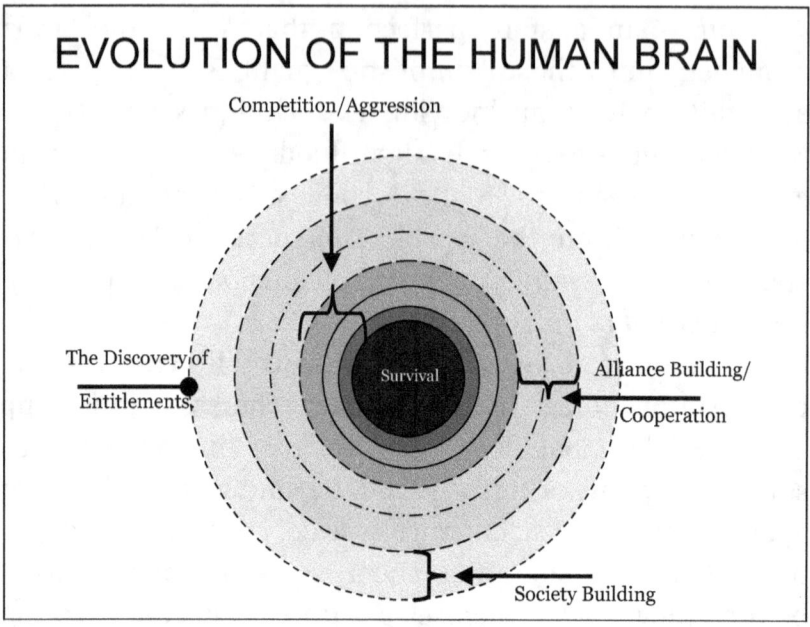

Figure 4. Evolutionary phases of the human brain. © R.J. Godlewski, "Human Intelligence: Perceiving an Enemy's Thoughts" *American Intelligence Journal 27, No. 1* (2009): 35.

The professional killer fails to reflect upon either killing as murder or his or her trade as extrajudicial. They have learned – or were born – to drop all emotional ties to their action and the target individual he or she has spent several months getting to know. They are not restricted by the proverbial love-hate coin that fuels both peace officers and terrorists. Inasmuch as a police officer risks his or her life to protect the innocent or a jihadist blows him or herself up out of, say, hatred towards Israel, the independent assassin merely conducts a trade. Death, for them, comes about as easily as a motorist might 'infringe' upon the speed limit or a shopper failing to report a minor undercharge.

A hired killer does not even exhibit emotion when considering the technique through which he or she is likely to suffer the target individual. Part of this rests with survivability – too much preference given to a particular method of murder will attract the attention of law enforcement. Part of it rests with efficiency – all preplanned murders remain different, as no two human personalities are exactly alike. Yet, one cannot dismiss the notion that since assassins achieve a near-perfect disconnect with the act of killing an individual, that he or she is likely to avoid attributing any degree of emotional respect towards the victim. Much the same could be said of a hunter that would not dream of injuring a family pet or poach during the offseason.

Considering Figure 4, we can reasonably conclude that independent assassins have emerged from competition and aggression ("routine" murder), but have not fully endorsed the alliances and cooperation of organized criminal assassins. Here rests an individual not afraid to take a life, but for whatever reason remains too frightened or inconsiderate enough to share the crime. The presumed nature of the crime – that of being a highly orchestrated, emotionless murder of an individual heretofore completely unknown to the killer – suggests a psychosis exhibited by many serial killers.

Even the infamous and as-of-yet-unsolved murders committed by Jack the Ripper in 1888 involved the killer fully announcing his exploits to both the police and the press.[61] This suggests that those who do not wish for their murders to become known as "murders" represent an entirely different breed. Everyone else, whether maniacal Victorian butchers or modern day *Los Zetas* thugs, employs the concept of using "terror" to some degree leaving independent assassins as, perhaps, the most honest of humanity's murderers. That is,

---

[61] Jonathan Ogan and Laurence Alison, "Jack the Ripper and the Whitechapel Murders: a Very Victorian Critical Incident" in Laurence Alison, ed. *The Forensic Psychologist's Casebook: Psychological Profiling and Criminal Investigation* (London: Rutledge, 2005), 23-46.

assassins simply kill and for a fixed, "no cure, no pay" fee. Add to this that he or she is likely to spend *months* analyzing a particular assignment before accepting the contract and their all "business-like" attitude remains astounding.

In Roger's case, this sense of omnipotent indifference to human beings led to his discharge from the military, presumably for the reasons indicated earlier: even the best warriors bear scruples. Similarly, in the case of modern street gangs, members are recruited to profit from a sense of affiliation and belonging, safety, identity, and, of course, recognition.[62] Ordinarily, Roger would have been a prime recruiting prospect for such gangs, but, perhaps, his refusal to fit in with *anybody* kept him out of necessary recruiting drives. In his case, he remained less of a professional assassin than a "lone wolf" pseudo terrorist.

Assassins, of the kind discussed within this book, represent people that can move through almost any society, pick up its habits and mannerisms, and, yet, venture out of the culture without being adversely affected by its idiosyncrasies (which could lead to discovery within virgin territories). Individuals such as Roger likely fall into Class IV and Class V terrorist profiles with ambitions, perhaps, for Class III mentalities.[63] It remains questionable on whether they could remain stable enough to locate the "reputable" clients that may find a need for an extremely discreet murder.

Any individual bordering between aggression and cooperation hovers within that netherworld where killing can take place (aggression) without the client becoming intimately involved with the action of the crime (cooperation). Usually, in civilized society, individuals that emerge fully into cooperation can lead towards peaceable communities whereas those hung up in competition/aggression trend towards incarceration. A

---

[62] McMains and Mullins, *Crisis Negotiations*, 390.

visual aid for this rests within the posturing (e.g., tattoos, etc.), on field antics (e.g., end zone dances), and, regrettably, public arrests of athletes whose particular sport remains little more than permanent competitive, aggressive allegiance. There is little inherently wrong with this as many non-athletes still engage within aggressive sports such as whitewater rafting, parachuting, hunting, karate, and a host of other activities.[64]

Professional assassins, contrarily, remain likely to suffer if they indulge within dangerous activities for the sake of danger. If, for instance, a professional football player, whose occupation requires physical battle with an opponent on the field, *still cannot whet his appetite for aggression*, what is the likelihood of an aggressive assassin remaining calm, cool, and collective during an eighteen-month long surveillance of a target? It remains, therefore, inconceivable that any professional assassin would engage within such activities as "ultimate fighting contests" – which Senator John McCain considers "human cockfighting" – that, amongst other liabilities, singles out the person as a trained fighter.[65]

We can remember the debate regarding special operations soldiers and hunters (Chapter 4); the assassin employs some *special methods* akin to elite military soldiers, but they remain isolated *from* the special operations community. Assassins *cannot associate with any group that most people consider a lethal organization.* Whether mixed martial arts (MMA) or SEAL Team 6, membership implies a need to strive for martial perfection along with ratification of accomplishment. In the case of the latter, an individual might as well hang a "trained to kill" diploma around his neck.

---

[63] Nance, *Terrorist*, 18-25.

[64] David A. Grossman, "Defeating the Enemy's Will: The Psychological Foundations of Maneuver Warfare" in *Maneuver Warfare: An Anthology*, ed. Richard D. Hooker, Jr. (Novato, CA: Presidio Press, 1993), 151-153.

[65] Couch, *Tactical Ethic*, 68.

Observing this, we can conclude that the professional assassin bears no such need for engaging within danger-loving activities such as rock climbing or bungee jumping. He or she *can* do these things – and may be so required to melt within a particular group – but does not possess a *need* to engage within any particular activity that may compromise his or her mental capacity. If this assessment is true – and all logic dictates this as so – then it supports the contention that assassins do not fall into cooperation or aggression, alliances or competition.

If our example of Roger failed to escape the notice of his military compatriots, it remains unlikely that he could survive very long as an independent assassin. His personality swung away from cooperation back into aggression too much to form the alliances (and hierarchy) that militaries require. He would never have reached that final stage of society building that soldiers desire and, instead, apparently sought to leap straight into entitlements – he *wanted* to be a special warrior, but did not earn his dues.

CHAPTER EIGHT: TRACKING THE GHOST.

John represented an enigma. His family thought him odd, while his critics thought him mad. Both groups, apparently, believed that the man just remained too factitious for his own good. Nevertheless, the Midwestern "oddball" possessed a gift, a talent most people could not fathom if their lives depended upon it and, mostly it did. What separated John from most other human beings remained his exceptional resilience, unfathomable memory, and primal senses. That is, John could smell things that others could not, hear things that others could not, see things that others could not, and categorized all into his mind for opportunistic recall later.

A natural physicist if not an academic one, John loved to figure things out and offer solutions to complicated problems. Sometimes he would "invent" things independently, only to later discover – to his mild discontent – that such innovations already existed within some remote laboratory or distant company. During other periods, he could literally predict the presence of individuals before he or she arrived or spontaneously declare the arrival of material ordered by those not affiliated with the man.

Such practical clairvoyance often tore at John's sensitivities. He could see "into the future" and yet could not *do so on a regular basis. Rather, such sensing came to him when he was rarely prepared for the visions. If he could only control his talents, he reasoned, he could do more for the communities that he served. Unfortunately, many of these populations wanted little to do with John. Some individuals even went out of their way to destroy his reputation or, at a minimum, did whatever he or she could do to tarnish his abilities out of abject jealously.*

Whatever the cause of critics' despicability, John remained living proof of the oldest dictum of human nature: the best athlete in the world may never have played a sport, the best musician never an instrument, and the best soldier never served within the military. John's Law, as known by a great many other principles, states that any one person is only as great as that which he or she desires to be. Opponents of this law merely object on the grounds that each individual must be "accepted" by all those within a given profession before he or she can claim to work within that particular field. John did not listen to the critics.

It remains a well-known fact that those with little or no formal education carried out some of the greatest achievements in human history.[66] Equally less remembered is the parallel that *everything* humans take for granted – science, medicine, music, business, etc. – arose from a singular individual who could not so much as find a position as a floor sweeper within that particular industry today. Perhaps, it remains those who dismiss this with the notion of education in favor of learning that allows some to achieve remarkable feats while others remain stagnated by the burdens of indoctrination.

To close oneself off to the prospects of human diversity

---

[66] See http://www.autodidactic.com/profiles/profiles.htm. Accessed October 2014.

force one to presume an intimate knowledge of what that diversity entails. In other words, those who preach diversity are often very intolerant themselves or, in the words of those like John, to fully understand the complexity of the human spirit requires one to fully allow his or her own spirit to flourish. This is why the *individual* remains the greatest threat to democratic bureaucracy ever known. To be human requires one to be both an individual and to follow certain rules of life.

Few can accept this irony, preferring to choose either individualism or institutionalism. On the one hand, the human person either can be *free* without regard to natural law or *freed* in regards to responsibilities accorded by that natural law. In brevity, either the individual person believes in freedom or free will – the former allows promiscuity while the latter requires trustworthiness. These distinctions warrant tremendous consideration in combating professional assassins, for the killer remains content to do as he or she pleases whereas the counter-assassin requires a lifetime of devotion in order to flush out the apparitional murders that remain the subject of this book.

Critics of this realization remain too segregated from the human mind to comprehend the Biblical edict to, "Train a boy in the way he should go; even when he is old, he will not serve from it."[67] Independent assassins only fear those who represent a lifetime commitment to track them down and take them out (or, possibly, incarcerate him or her). Eventually, even the most elite soldier in the world will retire, the most experienced intelligence operative fading away into post-government entrepreneurship at best. Neither is willing to devote fifty to one hundred years to stop, perhaps, a single individual. Yet, that remains the task of the professional counter-assassin.

---

[67] Proverbs, 22:6, *NAB*.

What sane individual could do such a thing? Frankly, someone precisely like John; an individual that can remain in focus even when the closest family and friends declare him or her to be absolutely stark raving mad. *Who* else would cause a coldblooded killer to tremble? Who *else* could ignore the assassin's defensive apparatus and go for the jugular? Both law enforcement and military personnel, even the "best of the best", are largely part-time reactionary forces. Even those combating terrorism or drug trafficking organizations remain susceptible to political decisions.

Now the question must be addressed, why would *anyone* devote an entire lifetime towards catching a singular individual *at best*? Easy. To save human lives. Even if professional assassins were only to kill, say, three people within his or her entire career, these are three *people* that a counter-assassin could save if the murderer were stopped early enough.

Naturally, pure economics – and, perhaps, efficiency – dictate that most law enforcement agencies abandon any concept of training their officers on the implications of professional assassins. More money, resources, and public attention are diverted to such noticeable groups as narcotics dealers (and the decades long 'war against drugs'). There just are not enough resources to spend on "wild goose chases" to seize suspected contract assassins – if they can even be discovered.

Enter people such as John. They represent precisely the type of individual that sees his or her work as lifetime pursuits rather than the shift work accorded to law enforcement or deployments attributed to the military. Even Navy SEALS and Army Special Forces remain too regulated for the task as even elite military personnel function according to ratified doctrine.[68] Individual soldiers are unlikely to take care of themselves on the battlefield.[69] What is required remains more entrepreneurship against criminality.

Alexander Graham Bell brought telephony into the world with having attended only a few lectures.[70] Richard Branson emerged as the billionaire owner of Virgin Records and Virgin Atlantic Airways by choosing a lifestyle of business rather than formal education.[71] The Wright brothers propelled humanity into powered flight despite representing self-taught inventors.[72] And Walt Disney taught the world to laugh by using correspondence schools to learn to draw cartoon characters.[73] The list of people that taught the world rather than being taught him or herself remains too great to list here, but such personalities represent the very type of individual required to safeguard the planet from destruction.

Too often, we limit security to those particular individuals that have earned their stripes through law enforcement or military service. We even go so far as to ridicule those who do not possess elite military service. Sadly, however, special operations-type armies have consistently lost the wars – if not the battles – against Third World "amateur" soldiers since 1945. As the United States and its Western allies shift towards more specialized, technology-centric militaries, America's asymmetrical threats will trend towards employing *anyone* available to attack us. In the words of Michael C. Fowler, "The more we exclude people from a solution, the

---

[68] Poole, *Tequila Junction*, 169-172.
[69] Poole, *Tiger's Way*, 37-38.
[70] http://www.autodidactic.com/profiles/profiles.htm#Bell. Accessed October, 2104.
[71] http://www.autodidactic.com/profiles/profiles.htm#Branson, Accessed October, 2014.
[72] http://www.autodidactic.com/profiles/profiles.htm#Orville. Accessed October, 2014.
[73] http://www.autodidactic.com/profiles/profiles.htm#Disney, Accessed October, 2014.

more our enemies will include them if they can."[74]

With the vast diversity of security threats experienced today, the world *cannot* ignore the contribution from all individuals, including those they may feel uncomfortable dealing with. For example, the aftermath of the Pike and Church hearings within the United States following the Vietnam War largely decimated the ranks of the Central Intelligence Agency. In fact, President Jimmy Carter fired approximately 4,000 field operatives a year before the Iranian revolution inaugurated a decades' long battle against radical Islamists.

The legacy of the last two American wars, in Afghanistan and Iraq, is that private security companies/private military companies (PSC/PMC) represent the template upon which future wars are staffed and fought.[75] Nations no longer bear enough manpower or resources to engage the proliferation of violent, non-state actors. And, yet, the same has yet to be transmitted down to law enforcement despite the proliferation of militarized police forces. This must change if municipalities or states desire to catch independent assassins.

The question of "how" has to represent the greatest question and the one that most likely keeps governments from considering the prospects. How, exactly, does one catch a ghost? By anticipating and then examining their *presence* – the social interaction (and disruption) that all humans manifest upon them wherever they go. In other words, we do not seek out assassins; we comprehend their habitancy and send investigators such as John on their tail for the duration. To begin with, we must retreat to the discussion surrounding

---

[74] Michael C. Fowler, *Amateur Soldiers, Global Wars: Insurgency and Modern Conflict* (Westport, CT: Praeger Security International, 2005), 158.
[75] P.W. Singer, *Corporate Warriors: The Rise of the Privatized Military Industry* (Ithaca, NY: Cornell University Press, 2003), 49-70.

Figure 3 and follow a pattern of questions.

- ✓ Is the death directly suspicious or obviously natural? If the death appears natural, are there *any* extenuating circumstances designed to make the death appear ordinary? For example – and this would be the first order of business for anyone investigating a high profile celebrity's death – is the death attributable to the victim's personal lifestyle? Alcoholics, as but one example, present various opportunities to "stage" deaths, but he or she possesses a *specific* behavioral profile that others are not familiar with. An investigator understands that many gun collectors, for instance, rarely commit suicide with his or her firearm because they both understand what that weapon is capable of doing and many suicides do not wish to "soil" treasured assets.

- ✓ If the victim represents a high profile individual, then the death should automatically come under suspicion. In the case of business executives, anyone cable of running or founding a large enterprise is not likely to fall victim to "accidents" or "frivolous" behavior. On the other hand, celebrities and athletes rarely undertake activities alone. In the first case, anything that would make an ordinary citizen look foolish should draw a red flag. The caveat here is that children and grandchildren of successful business people often do such foolish things. In the second case involving actors, athletes, and other entertainers, there is little reason to suspect that a death would not be preventable if, say, they were driving high performance automobiles while drunk. If "He should have seen *that* coming" meets "Too good to be true", then investigators must conclude some measure of illicit activity. Freak accidents happen *only* in the mind, for there is usually a long series of misfortunes. "Cleanliness" is the work of a professional.

✓ What are the immediate implications of the death? Who benefits in wealth? Control? Peace of mind? Accidental deaths remain far too shocking for most individuals to consider "the future". Even grieving wives tend to focus more on sadness than concerns about survival. If anyone seems to profit handsomely – even outside of wealth, as in ridding oneself of an adversary – then there is suspicion. The conclusion that a crime may have been committed does not foretell of an assassin's reach, but does provide motive for murder. Where an assassin may arise is whether the crime in question remains a lengthy prospect. Remember, a professionally planned assassin is likely to take upwards of a year and a half to orchestrate. Most opportunistic murderers simply do not wait that long. Because of this, an investigator must *begin* digging backwards at least 18 months.

✓ How do the principals surrounding the victim behave? In a "traditional" murder, for instance, *someone* tends to behave suspiciously under questioning. In an assassination, if the crime was never made explicit to the client (the 'security' provision ruse discussed earlier), then he or she is likely to act truly dumbfounded despite complicity. An experienced investigator must find the blemish between suspicion and naiveté.

In consideration of the multitude of questions identified above, there may be something that distorts the image of a death in the same manner as an artist can detect flaws in masterpieces. Here is where local law enforcement *should* consider the possibility of an assassination conducted by an independent contractor.

To understand this, let us consider the following two cases:

> *Case #1*. A wealthy landowner is found floating face down in a river while fly-fishing on an extended holiday. He is survived by his elderly wife and five children. His business deals exclusively with condominium developments throughout the northeastern United States.

> *Case #2*. An athlete with a questionable moral reputation dies in an automobile crash, his vehicle leaving the road to descend into a deep ravine. He was just concluding a contract year with his team, though no definite agreements were made. He was single.

In each case, permit us to assume that an assassin was involved. What peculiarities might be uncovered to enable local authorities to suspect assassination?

The commercial developer in Case #1 offers several prospects. First, while his age could suggest a heart attack, this remains offset by the fact that his relative experience fishing would presumably keep him from falling into the river from an accident. An autopsy should rule out health conditions, but not accidents. If he were fly-fishing *in* the water – assured by his donning waders – then an accidental fall would have likely made him fall *backwards* owing to extra clothing on his back. An analysis of river current would determine the severity of being thrust over. We now turn to his heirs.

Five children generally do not squabble over

possessions or wealth *unless* they were born far enough apart to dispense with familial bonding. As for the wife, it remains unlikely for an elderly spouse to employ murder as "natural death" may only be a short period away. The victim's business, however, offers opportunities for adversaries. Real estate developments within the environmentally fragile eastern United States bring into suspicion a range of environmental groups, unions, politicians, etc. The best target individual would, however, be someone that the victim out bid or otherwise prevented from obtaining exclusive property rights. Environmentalists generally cannot afford assassins and unions tend to employ their own "aggressive" people.

Case #2 bears both notoriety and simplicity. Public figures with attitudes – good or bad – spark hatred amongst differing segments of the population. The truth being that both decent people and "vicious trolls" tend to ignore the unknown. Athletes, like entertainers, draw critics almost as well as politicians do. For an ordinary individual, crashing a sports car down a ravine would almost immediately be labeled as reckless driving down a curvy freeway. For the athlete or actor, however, there will *always* be some individuals who argue for conspiracy. Just consider the accident that took the life of James Dean as an example.

With no wife and no steady girlfriend, the athlete's death does not fall under suspicion of inheritance. *However*, his contract negotiations may be viewed from the material wealth perspective. Who benefited the most from his death? The team owner? His agent? Perhaps a powerful gambler that lost a great deal over his concentration on receiving a larger contract? This particular case remains extremely difficult to analyze because contract assassinations require an individual to pony up from several hundred thousand dollars to maybe even one million or more.

We can omit a disgruntled fan as well as any junior

players. With his poor moral character, we would have to dig into his life during the previous two years or so and discover what major indicators may rise. Were *all* his off-field activities licit? Was he about to testify regarding performance enhancing drugs? It remains unlikely that team ownership would have been involved because, at worst, his failure to accept a contract would have kept money in the hands of the corporation. People only get angry over *losing* money, not keeping it. The best focus rests not with the sport itself, but with the peripherals involved such as drug use, court appearances, or gambling debts.

The astute reader, however, would correctly assume that such illicit activities provide killers from associated groups. There would be no apparent need for a highly specialized independent assassin to "convince" a motorist to accelerate into a ravine. In this case, we have to consider the extraordinary conclusion that the athlete may have actually hired the assassin himself. While suicide-by-assassin suggests astronomical rarity, it cannot be dismissed completely. There remain a multitude of reasons for ordering one's own death – insurance, psychosis, depression, etc. – and the employment of an assassin may simply be a device to prevent the victim from becoming terrified over his or her own pending death. After all, suicide is often considered the coward's way out and if this psychological stereotype were true, then this scenario offers the best explanation.

However a local official becomes suspect regarding an assassin, the next step – by far the most costly and complex – is to track down the culprit. Here is where individuals such as John come into play for the effort would dwarf that of even the most dedicated "cold case" specialist. The mission now ventures outside the figurative jurisdiction of the municipality's resources and personnel. The counter-assassin remains a launch and forget investigator, someone capable of going after the murderer without ceasing as such crimes fall outside statutes of limitation.

An analytics-centric investigator remains likely to see the evidence of a particular crime and then formulate his or her strategy around those features. For instance, an individual working an auto crash will receive blood toxicology reports indicating that the victim was inebriated and proceed under suspicions of drunk driving. Very few would begin with the question of whether or not the driver was *forced* to drink the beverage because, unless one was a fan of 1959's *North by Northwest*, such an idea appears extremely remote within modern society. Police agencies remain too overburdened to consider *every* possible option.

Nevertheless, does society abandon enforcing the laws *when* an independent assassin arrives onto the scene? Of course not. Unfortunately, however, most assassin-related crimes undoubtedly end up in the cold case files along with the rest of the 6,000 unsolved murders in the United States each year. This is why law enforcement assets are not sufficient to flush out the murderer. A better option remains a standing reward for anyone that can aid in bringing the perpetrator to justice. A sufficiently large reward – cost effective compared with ongoing law enforcement investigations – will attract individuals such as John.

There will also be hordes of malcontents seeking the money, but these individuals will remain transitory and largely fade out before many are capable of disrupting the investigation. Contrarily, they may also be useful in driving out – or dogging, to use a hunting term – the assassin, preventing the individual from seeking refuge. Unfortunately, before most – if not all – municipalities suspect "assassin", the perpetrator of the crime will likely be on the other side of the planet seeking his or her next opportunity.

However odd an individual such as John may appear to

the disinterested, his qualities represent just the sort of individual that can track down an assassin – providing that there is some measure of monetary reward for his or her efforts. Perhaps, such enticements remain little more than the no cure/no pay arrangements that assassins themselves undertake. After all, what is the legitimacy in denying duplication of the murder's own business? In an era of private military companies fighting wars against non-state actors, where is the justification to dissuade private entrepreneurs from tracking down fleeing murderers?

Admittedly, this proposal stretches the imagination a bit, particularly from the perspective of municipal "government remains omnipotent" bureaucrats, but the fact that professional assassinations often go unsolved, there remains a definitely need to adjust conventional wisdom. We must remember individuals such as Ted Kaczynski, Eric Rudolph, and even Osama bin Laden that took a great many years of multi-agency effort to track down. How much easier would it be for a contract killer to escape when the local authorities inadvertently assume "accident"?

Perhaps the best way to track down the "ghosts" of privately sponsored assassinations remains to leave the field open for individuals to solve on his or her own. That is, when the world does not need another American Red Cross or United Way, some individual *somewhere* will determine that his or her "mission" in life remains to do whatever he or she can to track these apparitions down and bring them to justice. Someone like John would use his exceptional memory, pattern recognition, and creative thought to look past the evidence and see the implications of each piece of data.

As with any experienced intelligence analyst, they will "...play scraps [of information] into patterns...go out and get drunk and get laid and come back and play with them some more. Suddenly [they] see something. It hits [them] in the

head and belly" and a perpetrator's presence is realized.[76]
While such individuals may not represent the kind of person
that fathers would want their teenage daughters to date, they
represent the tenacity required to undertake the seemingly
impossible.

The first step in tracking down ghosts, after all, is to
believe in ghosts. The next step is to collect as much
information has humanly possible regarding the environment
and the "incident" in question. The third step remains to go
back into the victim's past at least a year and determine the
merits and detriments of his or her death. *This takes a
creative personality.* Few law enforcement officials seek
justifications from that far into the past, preferring instead to
work backwards from the date of the accident.

Individuals such as John have brought a great many
innovations in life, some memorable and others not. They
have laughed at convention and, ultimately, his or her ideas
became conventional thought. With the rapidly expanding
population and dwindling taxpayer-financed resources,
individuals will begin to represent both the problem *and* the
solution to the world's predicaments, including the tracking
and apprehension of independent assassins. In the immortal
words of Edmund Burke, "The only thing necessary for the
triumph of evil is for good men to do nothing."[77]

[76] Paul Balor, *Manual of the Mercenary Soldier* (Boulder, CO: Paladin Press, 1988), 229.
[77] http://www.brainyquote.com/quotes/quotes/e/edmundburk377528.html. Accessed October 2014.

AUTHOR'S POSTSCRIPT.

Writing a book on independent contract killers brings with it a host of problems, not the least of which involves the emergence of critics. There are those who question the ability of *any* author to write about such an elusive subject. These individuals are correct in the enormity of the task, but often forget about the associations that some people come across during the course of his or her life. A second group criticizes an author based upon "mirror imaging" – the intelligence term that describes imposing one's thoughts and beliefs upon another individual. Just because, say, one person believes that *only* a Navy SEAL or Army Green Beret can undertake extraordinary tasks does not preclude relatively untrained individuals from doing likewise.

A third group represents "trolls" that simply like to criticize for the sake of criticizing and rarely offer anything more valuable to society than inflating his or her online ego. To them, I say, if you cannot rest on your own laurels, then head back beneath the bridges of obscurity. I will only offer the first two groups some measure of my own background with which to gauge my book and career by. I feel that this is only fair as the reader has taken a portion of their valuable time to peruse my words and I always repay my debts in some fashion or another.

As previously stated, I wrote *Skills of the Assassin: Understanding the Tactics of the Professional Killer* for three distinct reasons, and they involve rarity, opportunity, and notoriety. That is, nobody else had, the government may not like, and why the hell not. No author really requires a foundational reason to write as we all simply do so because, yes, it is a gift. We have all seen people that lack this gift of prose – the aforementioned trolls comprising the final group of critics. No matter how talented or educated one may be, if you resort to insults to get your point across, then you lack the 'gift'.

As for myself, I do not necessarily enjoy writing, let alone designing book covers, publishing the book, and marketing the work. I merely do so because God has permitted me to write and this usually entails some measure of *His* will for the world. In this regard, I *try* to teach others "something" that may save his or her life – or at least benefit them in some measure. This broaches upon the second group's interests, but I am *not* writing for Navy SEALS or Army Green Berets. Our worlds – and beliefs – remain so far apart that both of us would probably find it offensive to share company. That said, I salute you for the brave work that you do around the world and in service to this greatest of nations on earth.

Perhaps the first group requires more attention at this time. How can *anyone* write about independent, professional assassins? Pretty much the same way that people write about any other subject: with an open mind and common sense. Growing up in Michigan during the 20th century was not as uneventful as most people would believe. My family, it is told, swirled within the ranks of the notorious Purple Gang that terrified even Al Capone. My uncles and father even formed their own street gang. It was a very violent period and I still laugh, to this day, over hearing how none other than Jimmy

Hoffa himself once bailed my father out of jail. And here I thought that my dad and mom (whose own parents made bootleg liquor) led boring lives.

During the infamous summer of 1967, we lived on Detroit Avenue not far down the road from the riots erupting in the Motor City and for which required federal paratroopers to quell. Even before I enlisted within the Navy at 17 (turned 18 before all the paperwork was processed, however), I knew that the world was a very dangerous place in which to live. My second-grade classmate was brutally murdered by her uncle and I still remember them searching the neighborhood for her body. In kindergarten, my best friend was born without arms. Yes, I knew that the world was not convenient.

Serving at Pearl Harbor during the early 1980s allowed me to encounter all sorts of disreputable people, most of who were left over from the Vietnam conflict. In some of the notoriously shady bars that I used to frequent in my youth, were former members of MACV-SOG and current members of the CIA and its Soviet rival, the KGB. I long since forgot how many drinks were bought for me, but I sometimes wonder *who*, precisely, bought them. No matter, I was a low-level electrician and one thing that Godlewski's are well known for, is our ability to hold liquor. Which probably explains why my dentist had to shift from Novocain to sodium pentothal, but I digress...

For all the diversity of humanity and nation-states, there are relatively two distinct groups of people on the planet: those who believe they understand the world and those who remain shocked over just how horrible the shadowy portions of it are. There is far more to stormy weather than meets the eye. The same rests with human interaction. I learned this through the chance encounters that filed away within my mind for future recovery. After time, they built up into complete pictures with very little input from my imagination beyond realizing how Tidbit A connected to Tidbit D.

In the three decades since my active naval service (did time in the reserves, but outside of our "going on alert" during that brief coup attempt in Moscow while training in August 1991, nothing extraordinary occurred during that service), I have been able to build up contacts and associations that supported what I had learned in the Navy. No matter whether it is in Japan, Korea, Philippines, Canada, Mexico, Brazil...people *learn* things. Having lived within six U.S. states and routinely conducted business in forty-five, I can attest that what happens overseas does not *stay* overseas. Some of the most violent groups within the United States today exist in quaint little towns that bear no more than two police officers. Perhaps with good reason.

When you do not forget, you remember. And I remember thousands of statements and mutterings from the past five decades that *sometimes* add up to rather remarkable revelations. These occurrences permitted me to write these two books on professional assassins. I cannot disclose any more nor would I if I could. As for the 'why' in all of this, imagine what could have happened if *someone* had penned a book on crime scene preservation or forensics during the era of Jack the Ripper. If a person has done something in the past, then that is an excuse for me to do it. If someone has not done something in the past, then that is a *reason* to do it. Nobody had written a book about assassins – except alleged autobiographies and histories – and therefore my first reason for doing so.

Let us now return to the second group that believes that only elite military forces can undertake extraordinary actions. You are probably correct on that matter. However, how does one define "extraordinary"? If you mean HALO jumping out of an airplane over Iraq from 30,000 feet, then, by all means, label that feat as extraordinary. Yet, Navy SEALs do this all of the time, so *is* it extraordinary then for a SEAL? Or British SAS? Delta Force? Extraordinary is relative.

Again, as I have said, my life is relatively boring and lackluster. Some people view writing a book as "extraordinary". Others – myself included – only view such things as rising from the dead as extraordinary, but religion represents the scope of my *next* book. Not this one. I – and the rest of humanity – are painfully ordinary. Some people accomplish fantastic feats but do not serve within even the basic military. My paternal grandfather was one; at 5'2" and 120 pounds, he could bend spikes in half and once lifted an automobile by himself when my grandmother was trapped underneath it. Obviously not an SUV, but... Word has it that Buffalo Bill wanted granddad to work for him.

Still some within the elite military units – and their supporters – gaze down upon us four-and-out types as if we were never really in the military. Did I serve during an active war? Depends upon how you define a war. In 1983, I was overseas during both Korean Air 007's downing and the Marine Barracks bombing in Beirut. We arrived in the Philippines just as they were lifting martial law. If that was peacetime, I do *not* want to see war.

Regardless, if you ask if I have *ever* shot anyone, stabbed them with an improvised weapon, or engaged in unarmed combat with a drug-influenced thug at least three times my size, then, technically, I have to say yes (and I have already written about these occurrences). A disciple of the pre-Internet age, I have also learned how to stalk game as a child, how to literally pin-hammer my shots from extreme elevations, and recognize the difference between a blue jay and a bluebird by sound.

In grade school, we used to camp out on relatively remote (for eight-year-olds, half a mile is remote) islands *without adult supervision* and, living on an island, learned to operate almost every mechanical device or vehicle there was. In fact, my darling older brother, the *one* that wanted to join the Navy as a UDT member after watching countless shows with Lloyd Bridges during his youth, often sent *me* on "combat swimmer" missions along a nearby canal to egg the houses of disreputable neighbors during Devil's Night. After swimming back out, he would race the family's speedboat past me as I desperately tried to grab and cling to the inner tube strapped along the side. And they say that no human can swallow more than eight quarts of water...

No, my life is neither militarily significant nor extraordinary in any measure. I *do* know what it is like to be surrounded by fuel oil fires without protective clothing but that means very little in the grander scheme of things. I was a shipboard firefighter because I was the ship's electrician and that was my duty. *Everybody* pitched in, however, when events reminded us that the nearest dry land was thousands of miles away. None of this means that I cannot relate or understand diverse subjects, but I do understand my limits.

Just because I sensed what it was like to try to land a small plane in the slipstream of a Boeing 747 does not make me a pilot (it did, fortunately, convince me to take up scuba diving instead). Similarly, just because I know what it is like to sleep alone underneath a thunderstorm in the Amazon jungle does not mean that I am an explorer. Driving a tractor-trailer rig down a steep mountain in the dead of night with a full load of swinging beef while losing air pressure to the breaks is stressful, yes, but not like caring for a dying wife. These things remain relative.

Writing a new book on assassins, therefore, does not mean that I support professional killer nor does it imply that I know everything there is to know about the trade (otherwise this book would be several hundred pages longer). My purpose in life remains, always, to "Protect the dignity and integrity of innocent human life, wherever and whenever it may be placed into jeopardy and by whatever means may be necessary." It is not to join elite military forces or engage trolls in combative retaliation.

I, therefore, realize that there *are* limitations with modern, Western military forces and, frankly, no use for revenge writing. I write my niche books to engage the average citizen and concerned professional, *not* to discuss what *I* do. The reader must reach into his or her own soul and decide what *they* want to do to aid the world. My approach may not be sufficient or practical for them. Each of us bears our own talents, resources, and time.

The world is rapidly disintegrating around us and neither militaries nor governmental agencies appear willing or capable of defending human life. Mexico remains a failed state in waiting and most nations of the Middle East represent little more than Islamist tyrannies in disguise. Europe has long since passed its glory days and Latin American never possessed any. Asia's fascination with capitalism is transitory and nascent at best. As for the United States of America, four decades of political correctness have destroyed both the incentive and terminus for success.

In the midst of this chaos, individuals will still reign free to commit depravities of all variations. There are human traffickers, narcotics producers, forgers, anarchists, terrorists, and, of course, assassins of all persuasions. The subject of this book – the independent contract assassin – may indeed survive them all. Perhaps *you* will do something to stop them. Perhaps, you will simply do *nothing* and criticize others for trying to do whatever he or she can to protect the dignity of human life. After all, if the global media would have you believe, there are far more pressing issues such as wage inequality, discrimination (actually, preferential treatment) against women, and whether marijuana should be legal.

Some people, such as me, prefer to focus, not on the next fifty years, but on the next five hundred, one thousand, or more. We understand that civilization is what transpired during the past 25,000 years and not the previous 50. In the context of eternity, even the trillion plus year life of red dwarf stars pales in comparison. *This* thought is, perhaps, the only extraordinary thing that human beings can conceive of.

While I already spoke of my reasons for writing the previous *Skills of the Assassin*, this particular text was written for a *very specific* purpose – to let the world of villains know that *I* am on their trail, whether my professional associates join me or criticize me. In the grander scheme of things, I possess the endurance, resilience, creativity, and spirit that few elite soldiers possess. Where I fail in resources or training, I make up for in force multiplication. Since the passing of my beloved wife in 2003, I have long since lost the concept of fear, materialism, or convenience. I take what I have and use it for whatever purpose that supports my God-given mission.

Some may view *More Skills of the Assassin: Delving Deeper into Human Depravity* as merely a form of audacious self-promotion. Fine. Why would I promote anyone else? Who could fill my shoes? Whose shoes could I fill? Let us cease criticizing one another and join forces to rid the world of evil. Soon, I expect to retire on the plains of Africa to safeguard our planet's animal life from poachers and other malcontents. Somewhere on the planet earth, there will be *someone* who will pick up where I have left off and, collectively, we shall have made the world a better place in which to live. Remember, the only thing for the triumph of evil...

[Enough blood has been spilt]

MATTHEW 13:57

APPENDIX A. HUMAN VULNERABILITIES.

In discussing the context of independent assassinations, one has to consider the various methods of killing an individual without raising suspicions. Without going to extreme detail – this book was never meant to teach you *how* to kill for there are several books and documents online that already do so – a brief discussion can aid the uninitiated in determining whether foul play may be involved. To the degree that the investigator builds upon his or her knowledge, these "critical areas" can stimulate further reading and learning.

The sensitive areas of the body range from critical (broken spinal cord) to influential (poisoned digestive tract) to differential (circulatory or respiratory systems). Any one of these things can kill a person, but the time involved varies considerably. In the case of the independent assassin, the needs are quick enough to confirm a kill while lengthy enough to permit suspicion from arising.

The following photographs explore these areas upon the human body and illustrate potential vulnerabilities.[78] Discussion on precise methods of death will continue in the next appendix. These diagrams are for informational purposes

---

[78] Photographs © AlienCat - Fotolia.com.

only and do not represent acute medical knowledge.

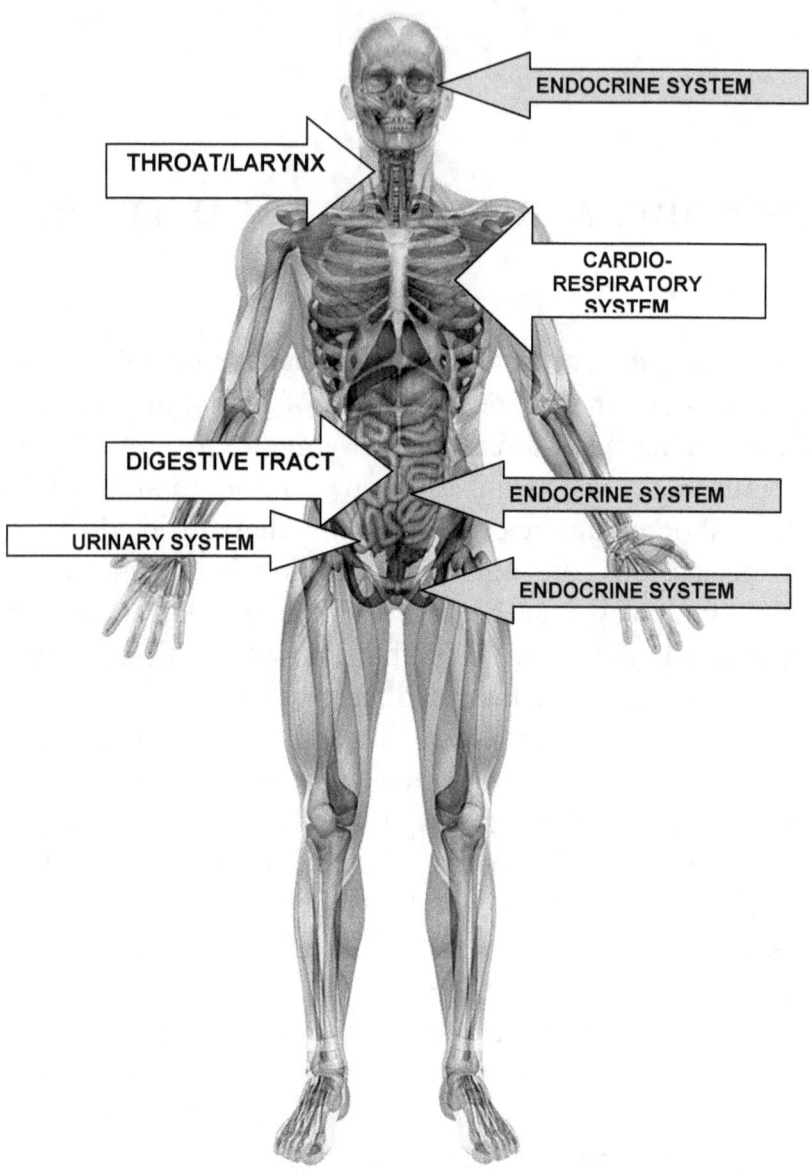

Figure 5. Vulnerabilities of the human body (organs).

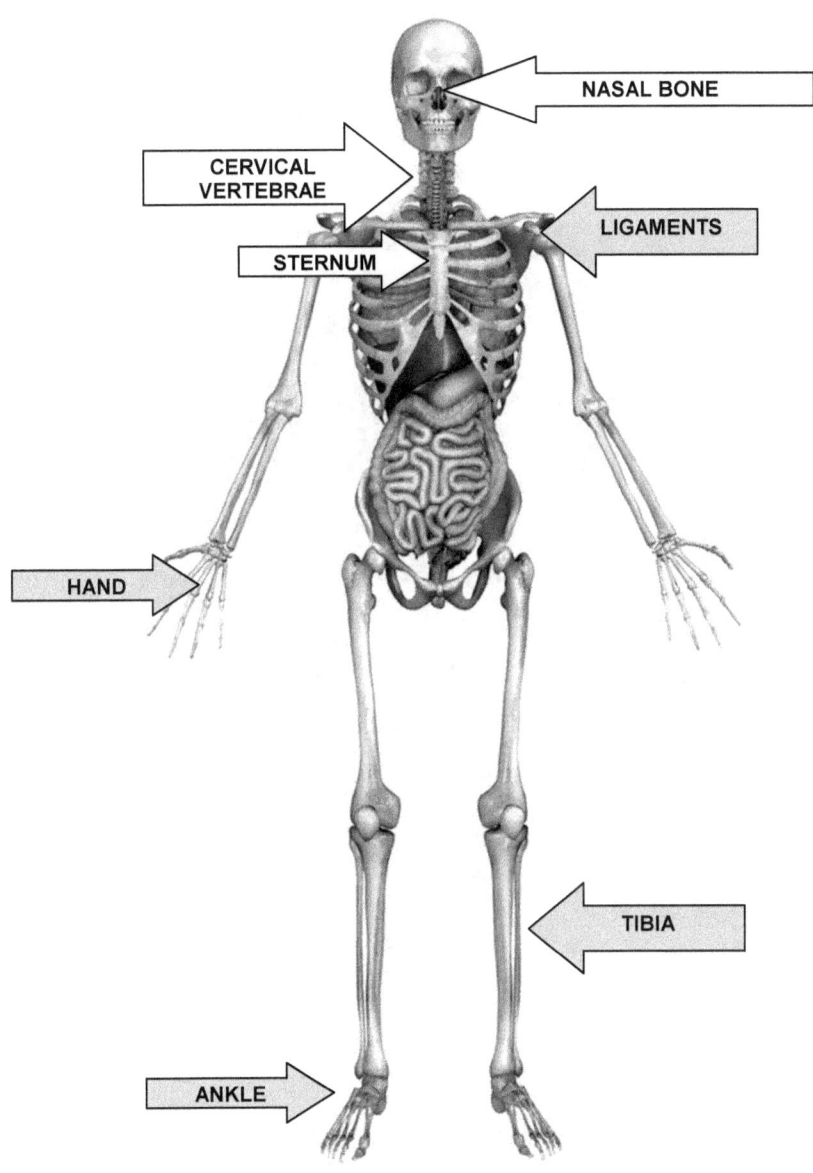

Figure 6. Vulnerabilities of the human body (skeletal).

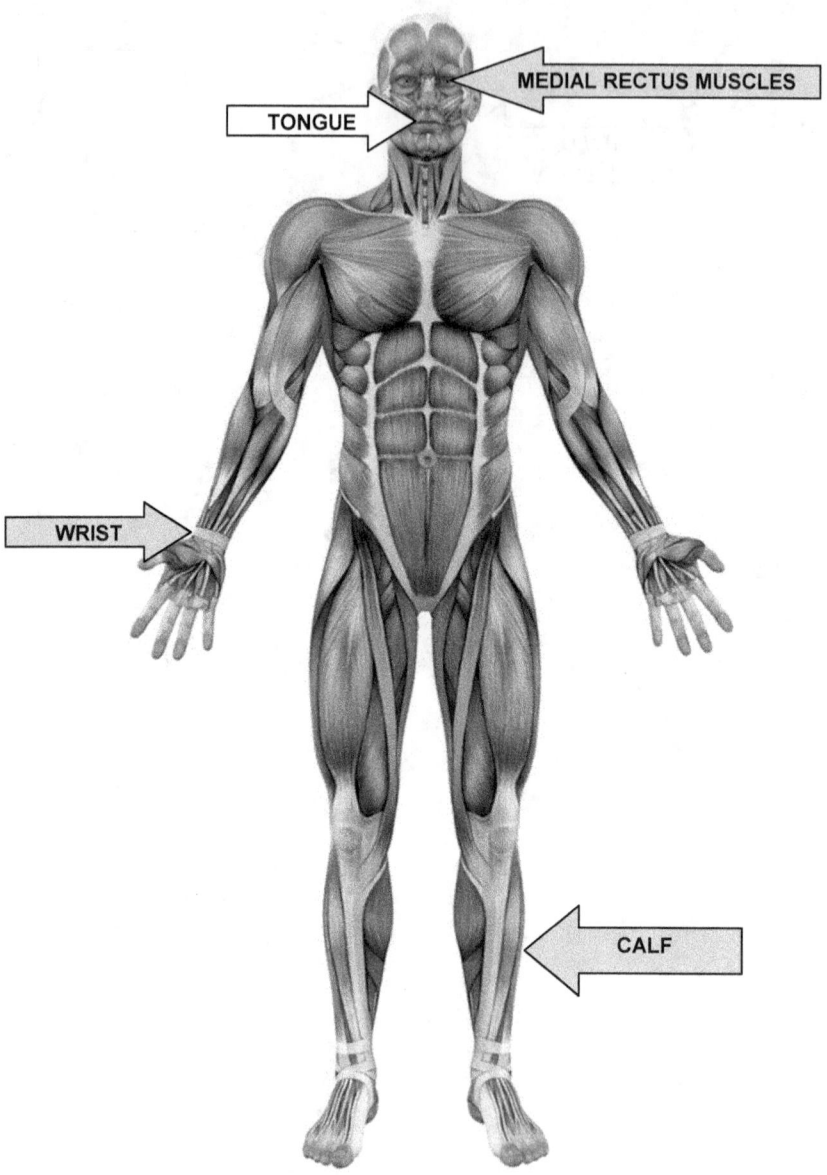

Figure 7. Vulnerabilities of the human body (muscular).

APPENDIX B. INNOVATIVE DEATH.

While it is known that death may occur in literally thousands of ways, the assassin is merely interested in the most effective manner that will allow him or her to escape connection to the crime. This may involve something as "simple" as providing Succinylcholine to a recuperating crash victim (nobody suspects assassinations *in* hospitals), or as "complex" as encasing a firearm's hammer in ice so that a victim commits "suicide" as soon as the ice melts. Mostly, however, assassinations occur through perceived accidents more than deliberate violence.[79]

In this section, we will briefly discuss how a professional contract killer may initiate such accidents or otherwise formulate an unsuspecting victim's untimely demise. Such murders can be classified into chemical, biological, and mechanical methods of introduction (concentration placed upon cause of death whether expeditiously or patiently). Examples include toxins (biological), medications (chemical), and, of course, firearms (mechanical). Some deaths may employ two or more of these categories, such as when toxins or medications cause an

---

[79] Source for medical information: U.S. Department of Defense, *Emergency War Surgery, Third United States Revision* (Washington: Department of Defense, 2004).

individual to fall down a flight of stairs.

For informational purposes only, such crimes may include:

Biological. There remain several methods of introducing biological toxins into the human body that may result in death. Al-Qaeda instructs its follows to introduce human feces into food, which is similar to the Vietcong dipping punji sticks into human waste to cause horrible infections within their victims. Human feces remains, arguably, one of the worst infection-causing agents known to civilization. Other groups such as the followers of Bhagwan Shree Rajneesh in Oregon employed salmonella, which if orchestrated upon a singular individual would pass as a rather unfortunate case of food poisoning.

Susceptible areas of the body include the endocrine system that includes all of the human glands and hormone producers; the cardio-respiratory system, which can offer either the heart or lungs as specific targets; the digestive tract; and the urinary system. In addition to death, these vulnerabilities offer a range of "accident-producing" options for the assassin. For instance, administering Benadryl® to an elderly person with a urinary tract infection can cause severe delirium, particularly at night.

The intention of using biological methods is to either cause incapacitation or confusion within the target individual. A person suffering from cramps while swimming or freestyle rock climbing may become just as dead as someone shot at close range from a shotgun. Furthermore, biological agents permit the assassin to travel further from the crime scene than either chemical or mechanical methods. The (presently) infamous Ebola virus, for example, possesses a 21-day incubation period. A victim may never remember where he or she became ill just that they are.

Chemical. Virtually every part of the human body remains susceptible to chemical solutions and compounds. Acids and bases destroy tissues, gases prevent the lungs from consuming oxygen, and medicines counteract the brain's normal functions. Anesthetic compounds disorientate the individual leading to, perhaps, mechanically induced deaths, and allergens can cease the functions of the heart and lungs. Vesicants can make the victim wish he or she were dead.

Certain relatively minor agents that attack the lungs mimic the conditions of pneumonia, if the assassin wanted to risk the findings of an autopsy. Nevertheless, not all incidents would automatically warrant post-death medical procedures. A victim that "accidentally" dosed his eyes with acid and proceeded to fall down a flight of stairs would not necessarily warrant an autopsy. After all, dead men tell no tales. Of course, the assassin would have to orchestrate such a maneuver – say, with a heavy drinker whom others would not question involving himself in such a "klutzy" death.

Mechanical. Machinations, undoubtedly, represent the majority of mechanical assassinations, but we cannot rule out deliberate measures such as gunshots, vehicular accidents, and simple strangulations. The key here rests usually with the vertebrae, though any number of other bone "breakings" will lead to the same conclusion. The point here is to employ _leverage_ to literally tip the scales in favor of the assassin. Any barrier or damage to the tibia will cause the victim to collapse awkwardly. Damage to the hands will forfeit a grip. Teeth and the nasal bone could project into the brain.

A crushed sternum may send rib "shrapnel" into major organs. Destruction of any vertebra can cease life, although if the fracture is too "clean" then suspicion is likely to develop. Falling down the stairs, contrarily, is usually a bit messier. However bones are broken, the injuries must _fit_ in with the

crime scene if accidents are the intent. A broken arm with a
.45 ACP slug in the humerus looks quirky.

Speaking of firearms, there is nothing in the assassin's
rulebook that prevents the use of guns to kill others. Merely
that shootings automatically involve the police. This said, a
long-range shot from a suppressed rifle employing frangible
ammunition would offer little forensic evidence. However,
even close-up shootings rarely lead to deaths. There are only
two reasons for which an assassin is likely to employ a firearm:
one, to ensure that an otherwise unapproachable individual is
killed, and two, to feign a crime committed by another
perpetrator such as a gang member or disgruntled employee.

In the case of the inaccessible victim scenario, the
assassin is likely to possess the time to employ a bespoke
firearm (and ammunition) that will not register on any federal
database. In the feint, the weapon will likely represent a
generic firearm, perhaps acquired through clandestine
sources, which will be disposed of once the crime has been
committed. In either case, the police are stopped in their
tracks or led on a series of questionable leads involving prior
owners.

Next to falls, electrocutions represent a primary method
for contract killers. Several thousand people within the United
States are accidentally electrocuted annually with another
30,000 receiving non-lethal shocks. With planning, there
remains very little reason to suspect that that "accident" was
anything but. Electricity can arrest the heart, damage the
brain, torch the skin, and blind the eye. And the 120-volt
systems in the U.S. home rest amongst the most deadly of all
as their amperage remains just powerful enough to lock the
muscles.

ABOUT THE AUTHOR.

R.J. Godlewski (GOD LESS KEY) is the manager of Tactical Extractions, LLC, a threat resolution services company, and presently serves as the president of Roadsailor Security Corporation. He is a graduate of American Military University, holding an M.A. in Military Studies, Asymmetrical Warfare concentration and a B.A. in Intelligence Studies, Terrorism Studies concentration, both earned with academic honors. He further holds graduate and undergraduate certificates in Security Management and Explosive Ordnance Disposal, respectively. Mr. Godlewski is a veteran of both the U.S. Navy and U.S. Navy Reserve.

Also by R.J. Godlewski

"Financial Counterintelligence: Fractioning the Lifeblood of Asymmetrical Warfare", American *Intelligence Journal* 29, no. 2 (2011), pages 24-33.

"Latte Intelligence: The Divorce of Shock Creativity and Special Information Operations", *American Intelligence Journal* 29, no. 1 (2011), pages 70-79.

"Human Intelligence: Perceiving an Enemy's Thoughts", *American Intelligence Journal* 27, no. 1 (2009), pages 29-37.

"Cultivating Creativity within Intelligence Analysis", *American Intelligence Journal* 25, no. 2 (2008), pages 85-87.

Targeting Narco-Submarine Networks through Deep Penetration, Autonomous Maritime Irregular Warfare Units Operating within a Hunter-Killer Role [Thesis Reprint].

Fourth-Generation Corporate Security: Asymmetrical Warfare for Protective Services Professionals.

Mini-Manual of the Independent Counterterrorist, Third Edition.

Skills of the Assassin: Understanding the Tactics of the Professional Killer.

Of What Price, Heaven? Encountering God within a Highly Secularized Society.

www.ingramcontent.com/pod-product-compliance
Lightning Source LLC
Chambersburg PA
CBHW070153290526

45789CB00002B/757